1994

Medieval Sign Theory and
Sir Gawain and the Green Knight

Penitent Woman from the *Lambeth Apocalypse*

ROSS G. ARTHUR

Medieval Sign Theory and *Sir Gawain and the Green Knight*

UNIVERSITY OF TORONTO PRESS

© University of Toronto Press 1987
Toronto Buffalo London
Printed in Canada

ISBN 0-8020-5717-9

Printed on acid-free paper

Canadian Cataloguing in Publication Data

Arthur, Ross Gilbert, 1946–
  Medieval sign theory and Sir Gawain and the Green Knight

  Bibliography: p.
  Includes index.
  ISBN 0-8020-5717-9

  1. Gawain and the Green Knight. 2. Signification (Logic). I. Title.

PR2065.G33A7 1987   821'.1   C87-093277-2

This book has been published with the help of grants from the
Canadian Federation for the Humanities, using funds provided by the
Social Sciences and Humanities Research Council of Canada, and
from the University of Toronto Women's Association.

To my mother and the memory of my father

Contents

Illustrations

Preface

This work had its origins in an almost accidental combination of academic influences. At a time when I was attempting to convince a group of undergraduates that the *Gawain* poet was intensely concerned with the productive possibilities of controlled ambiguity, and when I was searching through the works of modern semioticians to find a model for explaining the poet's practice, I happened to find a short reference in Copleston's *History of Philosophy* to Peter of Spain and his distinctions between *significatio* and *suppositio*. Further reading in medieval logic quickly convinced me of the utility of the analytic method implied by this insight: for all medieval literature, modes of interpretation need to be placed in historical context every bit as much as theological beliefs and social attitudes. In the years that followed, other investigators have followed similar paths of research, but usually making use of the more innovative and exceptional practitioners of medieval logic rather than the basic works that have informed my study.

What follows is a description of my itinerary through this material as it relates to *Sir Gawain and the Green Knight*. I have selected, in addition to standard texts written in Latin, a variety of materials written in Middle English to show that the modes of thought in the school texts are congruent with the assumptions in more widely distributed vernacular works. In most cases translations have been appended to these quotations, not because they are in themselves linguistically complex or because I have anything new to say about their basic meaning but simply so that this book may be of use both to medievalists who study other national literatures and to beginning students in medieval English. If the modes of interpretation discussed here were as generally accepted as I believe, this study should be useful to scholars working on any medieval European literature, and if they were common knowledge among fourteenth-century undergraduates, there will be little here beyond the comprehension of their twentieth-century successors.

Every author owes debts that cannot be properly acknowledged in notes. I would like here to express my gratitude to those people without whose intellectual, moral, and spiritual support this work could not have been done: David Arthur, Ruth Arthur, Frances Beer, Anne Burnett, Michael Cummings, Penelope Doob, Denton Fox, Roberta Frank, Joan Gibson, Maruja Jackman, D'Arcy O'Brien, and my colleagues and students at York University.

Medieval Sign Theory and
Sir Gawain and the Green Knight

Introduction

A   THE PROBLEM

Sir Gawain and the Green Knight is strongly resistant to any explanation that relies on decoding. Our sense of loss, as readers, is so great whenever a critic attempts to translate the Green Knight into a simple fiend, or a contemporary squire, or Merlin,[1] when a particularly slippery word is replaced by a narrow gloss, or when the narrative as a whole is declared to be an allegory for this or that Christian mystery, that the rational response, 'It is not only this,' yields quickly to the emotional assertion we see all too frequently in the scholarly literature, that 'It is not this at all.'

Yet the weight of historical evidence establishes that the poem invites such criticism. Each new monograph or article reveals another modern mind at work on the material, finding both pleasure and meaning in aspects of the poet's work that we never suspected were there and that we might still be tempted to deny are there at all. This multivalence must by now be accepted as a fact of the text: no new method or approach will sweep away all previous interpretative work; no rigorous scepticism will succeed in convincing us that all the critical diversity is nothing but critical error.

Much of the scholarly debate over some passages in the poem can be seen as the confrontation of complementary reductions, fought out by critics who consider them to be mutually exclusive. If one philologist glosses a troublesome form according to an Old Norse etymon and a colleague argues instead for a Vulgar Latin root, a literary critic needs little imagination to find an artistic justification for ambiguity in the passage, and so transcend (or at least circumvent) the debate. Successful as such a procedure may be at the verbal

level in providing the reader with a more meaningful text, it is less
acceptable as a device for explicating the symbolism of the poem.
Reconciling the readings that see the Green Knight as the Lord of
Hades, Ralph Holmes, and Christ,[2] for example, would lead the critic
into an agnostic morass and suggest a degree of incompetence in
the poet at variance with the experience of every reader.

This type of criticism unfortunately prevents any possible co-
operation. Unlike the philologists, who, true to their etymology,
seem really to love the poet's words, the 'Green Knight is Christ'
critic and the 'Green Knight is John the Baptist' critic are constrained
to do no more than joust when they meet. They must deny the
open spirit of the poem and reject the work of their colleagues utterly
instead of incorporating it and furthering the scholarly process.
Even when taken singly, however, such readings are unsatisfactory.
When the critic has completed his work, the poem often seems
diminished or even trivialized, as the shimmering complexity of the
surface of the text is replaced by schematic patterns that are not
only less complex but also far less interesting.

Fortunately, our reluctance to accept such reductionist criticism
need not be left anchored in something as vague as the often-ex-
pressed feeling that 'true literature' should not be so treated. We have
ample evidence from the work of the *Gawain* poet that the full
detail of the text was important to him in a way that set him apart
from many of his contemporaries. If we compare, for example, the
poet's presentations of Noah and Lot in *Purity*, with their interest in
all the physical and social dimensions of the narrative, to the reductionist allegorizations of the *Glossa Ordinaria*, the extent of the gulf
separating him from such attitudes becomes quite clear:

> 'Noe vir justus.' Hic per actus suos significat Christum, qui ait
> Matth. xi: 'Discite a me quia mitis sum et humilis corde.' Solus
> justus invenitur, cui propter justitiam suam septem homines donan-
> tur. Justus quoque Christus et perfectus, cui septem Ecclesiae septi-
> formi Spiritu illuminatae in unam Ecclesia condonantur.[3]

> 'Noah, a just man.' This man, by his actions, signifies Christ, who
> says (Matt 11) 'Learn from me, for I am gentle and lowly in heart.'
> Noah alone was found to be just, and because of his justice seven
> men were given to him. Christ was also just and perfect, and to him
> seven churches illuminated by the sevenfold Spirit were granted,
> gathered into one Church.[4]

> Lot frater Abraham, justus et hospitalis in Sodomis, significat corpus
> Christi, quod in omnibus sanctis inter impios gemit, quorum factis
> non consentit, et a quorum permixtione liberabitur in fine saeculi,
> illis damnatis supplicio ignis aeterni.[5]

> Lot the brother of Abraham, just and hospitable in Sodom, signifies
> the body of Christ, which is active in all the holy in the midst of
> the impious, and does not consent to their deeds, and will be liberated
> from mixture with them at the end of the age, when they are damned
> to the pain of eternal fire.

Now while there is nothing in the text of *Purity* that would make it
absolutely impossible for a reader to make such an interpretation,
there is also nothing to support it against an alternate allegorization,
such as the one offered in an *Allegoriae in Vetus Testamentum*
once attributed to Hugh of St Victor:

> Lot ergo intelligitur fidelis anima; Sodoma, vita saecularis; Segor,
> vita conjugalis; mons, vita spiritualis; uxor Lot, carnales qui sunt in
> Ecclesia.[6]

> Lot means the faithful soul; Sodom, earthly life; Segor, conjugal life;
> the mountain, spiritual life; the wife of Lot, the fleshly ones who
> are in the Church.

All we can say about such readings is that, in the case of *Purity*,
they would be extremely wasteful in that they ignore all the poet's
efforts to produce a striking naturalistic description of events important to his own world for more than abstract spiritual truths. The
case with *Patience* is, if anything, much stronger, since a reader who
insisted on approaching that poem according to the traditional
'Jonas, id est Christus' view would have to skip more lines than he
read.

   This attention to detail has not, of course, gone unnoticed, nor is
there any lack of attempts to explain the depth of meaning of such
surface material. Details of dress, physical appearance, colour, and
flora and fauna have all been decoded, often on the basis of solid
parallels in contemporary literature or, more frequently and more
readily, handbooks of symbolism. Since the poet was an educated
man living in an age when every object and quality in the world,
especially if it is mentioned in the Scriptures, was invested with a

moral and spiritual significance, it is only natural that a modern reader should try to understand *Sir Gawain and the Green Knight* on the basis of medieval ideas about the meaning of foxes, holly, pentangles, and green things in general. To this end a thousand years of Latin literature has been scoured in hopes of finding authoritative glosses and explications for the stubborn details of the poem.

Here too the decoding critics come to an impasse, and here too the root of the problem is a reluctance to learn from the false starts and the slow recoveries of the linguists. Reliance on the medieval handbooks is risky, since the various writers on the meaning of such signs do not often provide us with uniform explanations. Earlier writers differ from later; vernacular writers differ from Latin authors; and the same object may be interpreted *in bono* or *in malo* depending on the circumstances or, it seems, on the whim of the interpreter. If modern critics take any particular decoding of a sign as authoritative because it comes from a contemporary source, we are in danger of falling into the same arbitrary frame of mind, and open to the charge that we have been reading too selectively. If we argue, on the basis of one version of the *Secreta Secretorum* and its teaching about the connections between physiognomy and psychology, that the Green Knight's red eyes (line 304) mean that he is 'coraious, stalworth and myghty,'[7] we have no defence and little possibility of reconciliation with those who would say, on the basis of another version of the same text, that it is men with camel-coloured eyes who are courageous and that red-eyed men 'ben dysposed to woodnesse, y-likenyd to bestes whych may not be daunted.'[8] It seems likely that both contemporary and modern readers would make their choice of gloss on the basis of an already formed opinion about the Green Knight, not on the basis of belief in the authority of a particular physiognomic system.

The complex and self-contradictory nature of the tradition would seem to leave us once again on the edge of a critical, or rather uncritical, agnosticism, unable to make persuasive distinctions between acceptable and unacceptable interpretations. Our choice would seem to be between accepting the flood of Tantric, Hermetic, and Jungian explications and deciding that interpretation of such symbols should not be attempted at all. This feeling seems to be shared by Bloomfield, who says 'One has only to look at the *Distinctiones*, those symbolic dictionaries chiefly of the twelfth century, to see that there was no science of symbolism. The commonest objects and animals embrace a wide variety of meanings, often contradictory. The meaning could be interpreted only in context, if at all, and even then multiple interpretations would frequently be possible.'[9]

The fault is not (how could it be?) with the medieval texts, but with the use we have tried to make of them. We have long since discarded the notion, in our own dictionaries, that words can be explained by simple substitution of lexical 'equivalents' for the words of another language or for English words of another time. The failure of such attempts is obvious and has led to an increased so-phistication in theories of meaning. The study of other signs and symbols requires a similar rethinking of procedures, so that we derive from medieval texts the kind of information they are capable of providing, instead of faulting them for not giving us what we want.

It would be wasteful indeed to abandon attempts to understand the meaning of symbolic objects in *Sir Gawain and the Green Knight* just because the medieval texts do not line up with our notions of how signs function, and it is not acceptable to allow any and all explanations the same status regardless of their source, just as it would be foolish to abandon attempts to understand individual words or to treat them as interpretable at whim. The poem gives strong indications that some of the objects it mentions are to be taken not simply as objects included for their own sake but rather as signs for other things. Explanation of such signs as the pentangle, the picture of the Virgin, the green girdle, and Gawain's wound must therefore proceed, and it should follow a pattern responsive to medieval theories about signification.

While it is true that there was no 'science of symbolism' in the period, if by 'science' we mean a discipline that creates the equiva-lents of logarithm tables and lists of metallic specific gravities, the educated reader and writer of the period had access to a consid-erable amount of material about signs and their functions. Once we take seriously the possibility that our forebears were concerned with such matters, we find evidence of a pervasive theory of meaning that was not only directly available to the educated but also played an important part in shaping the view of the world found less overtly in writings in a wide variety of genres. In addition to the explicit formal system, found in the elementary writings on logic that formed a basic part of every scholar's education, contemporary works on heraldry and various sermons and doctrinal pieces relied on implicit knowledge of similar principles. It is to this system of meaning, as well as to parallels in specific content, that we must look in order to understand the roles of the *Gawain* poet's signs in their original social context.

Even the possibility of *in bono* and *in malo* interpretations is not the stumbling block it first appears to be. The existence of multiple meanings for individual words or visible symbols was not seen as a bar to understanding by medieval thinkers, and they were far from ill equipped to deal with them. Instead of focusing on the difficulties the phenomenon causes for our 'one word, one meaning' preconceptions, we would do well to recognize that controlled ambiguity was considered potentially productive of more (and more useful) knowledge. Augustine, in one of his most widely known and influential works, laid the foundation for a systematic approach to the creative possibilities inherent in the multivalence of signs:

> Huius igitur uarietatis obseruatio duas habet formas; sic enim aliud atque aliud res quaeque significant, ut aut contraria aut tantummodo diuersa significent. Contraria scilicet, cum alias in bono, alias in malo res eadem per similitudinem ponitur, sicut hoc est quod de fermento supra diximus. Tale est etiam, quod leo significat Christum, ubi dicitur: *Vicit leo de tribu Iuda*; significat et diabolum, ubi scriptum est: *Aduersarius uester diabolus tamquam leo rugiens circuit, quaerens, quem deuoret* ... sic et alia plurima ... Quando autem ex eisdem scripturae uerbis non unum aliquid, sed duo uel plura sentiuntur, etiam si latet, quid senserit ille, qui scripsit, nihil perculi est, si quodlibet eorum congruere ueritati ex aliis locis sanctarum scripturarum doceri potest ... Ille quippe auctor in eisdem uerbis, quae intellegere uolumus, et ipsam sententiam forsitan uidit et certe dei spiritus, qui per eum haec operatus est, etiam ipsam occursuram lectori uel auditori sine dubitatione praeuidit, immo ut occurreret, quia et ipsa est ueritate subnixa, prouidit. Nam quid in diuinis eloquiis largius et uberius potuit diuinitus prouideri, quam ut eadem uerba pluribus intellegantur modis, quos alia non minus diuina contestantia faciant adprobari?[10]

This variation takes two forms. Thus one thing signifies another thing and still another either in such a way that the second thing signified is contrary to the first or in such a way that the second thing is entirely different from the first. The things signified are contrary, that is, when one thing is used as a similitude in a good sense and in another place in an evil sense, like 'leaven' in the above example. This is the situation where the lion is used to signify Christ, when it is said, 'The lion of the tribe of Juda ... has prevailed,' but also signifies the Devil, when it is written, 'Your adversary the devil, as a roaring lion, goeth about seeking whom he may devour' ... Many other things are used in the same way ... When, however, from a single passage in the Scripture not one but two or more meanings are elicited, even if what he who wrote the passage intended remains hidden, there is no danger if any of the meanings may be seen to be congruous with the truth taught in other passages of the Holy Scriptures ... For the author himself may have seen the same meaning in the words we seek to understand. And certainly the Spirit of God, who worked through that author, undoubtedly foresaw that this meaning would occur to the reader or listener. Rather, He provided that it might occur to him, since that meaning is dependent upon truth. For what could God have more generously and abundantly provided in the divine writings than that the same words might be understood in various ways which other no less divine witnesses approve?[11]

The importance of this passage and the attitude it reveals is not simply in its tone, although it is significant that the situation that modern commentators treat as a cause for despair seems to Augustine a cause for delight. It is also an indication that centuries of this kind of analysis of words and other signs with multiple meanings had prepared the way for a very sophisticated attitude towards ambiguity by the time of the *Gawain* poet. It is possible to show that the poet has the same ability to deal with several levels of meaning as do the more formal language theorists of late medieval Europe. Just as they are more interested in the complexities of natural sign systems and with *modes* of meaning than in providing static lists of signs and their equivalents, the *Gawain* poet was interested in structuring various possible responses to his poetic material in terms of a doctrinally correct hierarcy of meanings. He is much more interesting to us, in addition, as a poet with a sophisticated view of signs and meanings than as a practitioner of symbolic shorthand, merely saying 'red-eyed' when he means 'courageous' or 'Green Knight' when he means 'fiend.'

B   THE TOOLS FOR ANALYSIS

It is Augustine, again, who provides the statement about the distinction between things and signs, *res* and *signa*, that is basic to any discussion of sign theory in medieval writings. Early in the *De Doctrina Christiana* he explains that

> Omnis doctrina uel rerum est uel signorum, sed res per signa discuntur. Proprie autem nunc res appelaui, quae non ad significandum aliquid adhibentur, sicuti est lignum lapis pecus atque huiusmodi cetera.[12]

> All doctrine concerns either things or signs, but things are learned by signs. Strictly speaking, I have here called a 'thing' that which is not used to signify something else, like wood, stone, cattle, and so on.[13]

Some such 'things,' those mentioned in the Old Testament, are also signs, but a general distinction may still be made between things and signs:

> Ex quo intellegitur, quid apellem signa, res eas uidelicet, quae ad significandum aliquid adhibentur. Quam ob rem omne signum etiam res aliqua est; quod enim nulla res est, omnino nihil est; non autem omnis res etiam signum est.[14]

> From this may be understood what we call 'signs'; they are things used to signify something. Thus every sign is also a thing, for that which is not a thing is nothing at all; but not every thing is also a sign.[15]

The importance of this distinction and the centrality of sign theory to medieval thought may be seen from the fact that Peter Lombard chose to open his *Sentences*, which was to become the universally accepted starting point for the discussion of Christian teaching, by quoting Augustine's words on the topic.[16] Nevertheless, Augustine's explanation was in later ages considered far from complete and needed to be supplemented with a great deal of other material from the philosophical tradition. A fourteenth-century Englishman with the general educational background we may safely ascribe to the *Gawain* poet would also be aware of other works on signification, dealing with problems concerning the establishment of signs,

their relationship to each other in propositions, and the nature of
the connection between a particular sign and its referent. These
works, widely known in their own day but now studied only by
specialists, provide important background material for the study of
the general theory of meaning in medieval writing, though they
offer very little in the way of lists of specific parallels in surface
content to the literature of the age.[17]

It is convenient to discuss the general ideas of meaning in the
system of late medieval writers according to four different points of
view. These do not form a strict logical hierarchy of mutually
exclusive categories but rather are different approaches that may be
selected in turn in order to understand the various levels on which
a particular sign actually functions. The first and simplest consideration is the realm of pure signification, the area that today would
be called lexical semantics. From this point of view a word simply
means what it means. There is considerable debate in this period
over whether the word signifies the thing itself or the mental image,
which in turn signifies the thing,[18] but in both cases the relationship
between sign and referent is one of simple equivalence, and the
sign is merely the substitute in discourse for the object in the world.
This approach is appropriate for simple dictionaries or foreign-
language phrase-books. For all its simplicity, however, it should not
be overlooked in analysis of poetic symbols; indeed, much of the
purpose of the pentangle and the green girdle in *Sir Gawain and the
Green Knight* is missed if we fail to examine their full implications
when considered *in vacuo*, in terms of their pure signification.

The second area of analysis revolves around the power of a sign to
cause an idea to come into the mind of the person who perceives
it. Augustine says

> Signum est enim res praeter speciem, quam ingerit sensibus, aliud
> aliquid ex se faciens in cogitationem uenire.[19]

> A sign is a thing which causes us to think of something beyond the
> impression the thing itself makes upon the senses.[20]

It is this property of words that allows him to avoid the apparent
contradiction that occurs, for example, when he says that God is
ineffable:

> Et tamen deus, cum de illo nihil digne dici possit, admisit humanae
> uocis obsequium, et uerbis nostris in laude sua gaudere nos uoluit.

Nam inde est et quod dicitur deus. Non enim re uera in strepitu istarum duarum syllabarum ipse cognoscitur, sed tamen omnes latinae linguae socios, cum aures eorum sonus iste tetigerit, mouet ad cogitandum excellentissimam quandam immortalemque naturam.[21]

For God, although nothing worthy may be spoken of Him, has accepted the tribute of the human voice and wished us to take joy in praising Him with our words. In this way he is called *Deus*. Although he is not recognized in the noise of these two syllables, all those who know the Latin language, when this sound reaches their ears, are moved to think of a certain most excellent immortal nature.[22]

This aspect of language is referred to as the 'epistemological relation' by P.V. Spade,[23] who asserts that despite the variety of positions taken during the key logical debates of the fourteenth century, it was an unquestioned given for all sides and was certainly part of the general opinion about how words mean. The continuing importance of this to *Sir Gawain and the Green Knight* is clear from the fact that the key poetic symbols have often quite different effects on the minds of different people, whether characters in the poem or readers; the poet is not simply exemplifying the epistemological function of signs but examining the problems that arise when there is no agreement on what thoughts the sign initiates.

The third consideration in determining what a sign means is its propositional context. Medieval logicians were extremely sensitive to the fact that the meaning of a particular word in a given sentence was qualitatively different from the *significatio* of the same word in isolation. This sensitivity may not have led to a formal theory as powerful as those that modern linguists are able to create (a fact that causes some scholars to adopt a rather patronizing attitude towards the efforts that were made), but the *terministae*, 'unlike the Ancient (and Early Mediaeval) grammarians ... had a clear notion ... of the fundamental importance of the *proposition* as the verbal context that decidingly determines the actual meaning of a term. To denote that actual meaning of a term they introduced a new word: *suppositio*, to be distinguished from the meaning of a word by itself (*significatio*).'[24] This distinction, which de Rijk's work traces back into the twelfth century, was an integral part of all writing on logic in the fourteenth century. It allowed theorists to discriminate between what modern ordinary-language philosophers call 'use' and 'men-tion.' The word *man*, for example, is said to 'stand for' (*supponere pro*) something different in the proposition 'Man is a three-letter word' from what it stands for in the proposition 'Man is the noblest of animals.' More important, perhaps, is the distinction between simple supposition, which occurs in a proposition such as 'Man is a species,' and personal supposition, in which the term stands only for one member of a class: 'A man runs.' In this latter case the meaning of the word is more obviously context-sensitive: if the verb in the proposition is in the present tense, for example, the *suppositio* of the term is restricted to men existing at present. Lack of attention to this distinction between supposition and signification was (and still is) at the root of much fallacious reasoning, which can often be avoided simply by specifying the different objects for which a given term stands in different propositions. As we shall see, there is an analogous distinction to be made in the functioning of the pentangle and the green girdle in *Sir Gawain and the Green Knight*, for the poet uses them not only as static labels for timeless universal referents (*significatio*) but also as elements in 'propositions,' which make assertions that must therefore be examined for their truth-value.

The fourth dimension of a sign's meaning is its relation to a larger social context. Here again there is nothing like the thoroughgoing relativism of modern socio-linguistics, but the medieval logicians did show an empiricist interest, for example, in the way that even the mere location of a speaker may have a determining effect on the meaning of an utterance. De Rijk refers, for example, to a passage in an early thirteenth-century tract dealing with the nouns that refer to particular dignitaries:

> quando hoc nomen '*episcopus*' per se sumatur cum verbo presentis temporis, suppositio non fit pro quolibet appellato illius dictionis, sed *pro appellato illius terre in qua profertur propositio*. Unde si quis Anag(n)ie dicat: '*episcopus venit*,' non est admittenda nisi pro episcopo Anag(n)ino. Similiter si quis dicat in Francia: '*rex venit*,' non est admittenda nisi pro rege Francie.[25]

> When this word *bishop* is taken for itself with a verb in the present tense, there is not *suppositio* for just any referent for the word but rather only for the appropriate referent of that land in which the proposition is uttered. Therefore, if someone in Anagni says, 'The bishop is coming,' it is to be accepted only of the bishop of Anagni.

> Likewise, if someone says in France, 'The king is coming,' it is to be accepted only of the king of France.

Roger Bacon gives a similar example to demonstrate the utility of a definite article. In the French proposition 'li reis vent,' the article is sufficient to show that the king in question is the reigning king of France.[26] Similarly, medieval writers used the word *philosophus* alone to designate Aristotle and *apostolus* for St Paul, confident that the full context of writer, content, and reader would prevent any misunderstanding of the words' *suppositio*.

These specific examples of sensitivity to context are, however, just a part of a larger general attitude towards language and its function current throughout the medieval period and attested in a wide variety of materials. Enlarging on the belief that the sign is a sign if and only if it produces an idea in the mind of a perceiver, Augustine in the *De Magistro* argues that it is of primary importance to know the intended audience if we wish to understand the meaning of an utterance. After a few pages in which he leads Adeodatus to a greater comprehension of human communication, he asks for a summary. Adeodatus not only provides a general explanation of the reason why we speak but also proceeds to repeat the modifications to the theory necessitated by two apparent counter-examples:

> AUG Iam quae sermocinando inuenerimus, uelim recenseas.
> AD Faciam quantum possum. Nam primo omnium recordor aliquam-
> diu nos quaesisse, quam ob causam loquamur, inuentumque esse
> docendi commemorandiue gratia nos loqui, quando quidem nec cum
> interrogamus aliud agimus quam ut ille, qui rogatur, discat, quid
> uelimus audire; et in cantando, quod delectationis causa facere uide-
> mur (non sit proprium locutionis), et in orando deo, quem doceri
> aut commemorari existimare non possumus, id uerba ualeant, ut uel
> nos ipsos commonefaciamus uel alii commemorentur doceanturque
> per nos.[27]

> AUG I would like you to review the results of our conversation.
> AD I shall do the best I can. I recall, first of all, that we inquired for
> a time about the purpose of language and discovered that we speak
> either to teach or to recall. Even when we ask questions, we do
> nothing more than teach the person interrogated what we wish to
> learn from him. In the case of singing, what we are apparently doing

for pleasure is not the proper function of language. In praying to God, who cannot conceivably be taught or reminded of anything, our words serve either to remind ourselves or to enable us to remind and teach others.[28]

In order to understand the meaning of a prayer, therefore, it is necessary to know the nature of God, the addressee; otherwise, the whole purpose of the utterance would be misconstrued.

The author of *Dives and Pauper* raises a similar problem, closer in time to *Sir Gawain and the Green Knight*. This work, from the early fifteenth century, examines Christian doctrine and presents its rather ordinary solutions to various doctrinal difficulties in the form of a straightforward dialogue between an ordinary bourgeois and an exceptionally thorough cleric. Since it is a popular, vernacular work, its underlying assumptions, if not its precise conclusions, may be taken as indications of general attitudes in the period. At one point in the discussion the worldly interlocutor is troubled by the apparent implications of asking God for aid, and his spiritual adviser shows him how the qualities of the addressee modify our under-standing of the speech:

> DIUES Why bad þan Crist þat men schuldyn nout spekyn mychil in here preyere?
> PAUPER Crist bad nout vttyrliche þat men schuldyn nout spekyn mychil in here preyere, but he bad þat men schuldyn nouȝt spekyn mychil in here preyere as heþene men don, for þey wenyn þat God schulde nout heryn hem but þey spokyn mychil ...
> DIUES Why preye we to God with our mouth, syth he knowyth al our þouȝt, al our desyr and al our wil and what us nedyth?
> PAUPER For, as Y seyde fyrst, God wil þat we knowlechyn hym for our lord and knowlechyn our nede, þat we mon nouȝt don ne han noþyng withoutyn hym, whyche knowlechyng must be don with þe mouth, for Sent Powil seyth þat ȝif man or woman wil ben sauyd he must han ryȝt beleue in herte inward and knowlechyn it outward with his mouth: Corde enim creditur ad iusticiam, ore autem confessio fit ad salutem (Rom. 10:10).[29]

> DIVES Why then did Christ command that men should not speak much in their prayers?
> PAUPER Christ did not command absolutely that men should not

speak much in their prayers, but he commanded that men should not
speak much in their prayers *as heathen men do*, for they think that
God would not hear them unless they spoke much ...
DIVES Why do we pray to God with our mouths, since he knows all
our thought, all our desire, all our will, and what we need?
PAUPER Because, as I said before, God wishes us to acknowledge him
as our lord and acknowledge our need, that we may do nothing and
have nothing without him, for Saint Paul says that if a man or a
woman will be saved, he must have right belief inwardly, in the
heart, and acknowledge it outwardly, with his mouth: Corde enim
creditur ad iusticiam, ore autem confessio fit ad salutem (Rom
10:10).

Prayer to God is only a special case of a general interpretative
necessity. If we wish to understand any sign or grouping of signs, we
must consider not only the meaning in isolation, the meaning in
propositional context, and the effect on the mind of an ideal perceiver
but also the possibility of various receptions by various actual
perceivers. From this point of view interpretation is a much more
complex process than is generally realized by modern decoding
critics; fortunately, we have adequate guides in the theorists of the
age.

The end result of the application of all of these viewpoints to the
visible signs prominent in *Sir Gawain and the Green Knight* is a
fuller appreciation of the poet's ability to structure complex ideas
around the various levels of audience interpretation of such objects.
Signs such as the pentangle and the green girdle are capable of
being 'read' in a variety of ways, but instead of leaving us in a rela-
tivist quandary, the poet has succeeded in building a properly orthodox hierarchy of such readings. Further, it is possible to demonstrate
why a sign such as the wound to Gawain's neck becomes a stable
sign whereas the attempt to assign an unchanging *significatio* to the
green girdle proves to be a total failure – a failure more instructive
than the success of many another hero.

This focus on modes of meaning rather than particular signs also
expands the number and type of works that may be used to contex-
tualize the material presented in the poem. There are a great many
medieval texts, corresponding to one or more aspects of the pentangle's function in the poem and bearing on the interpretation of
other visible symbols in it, that have not been fully exploited in the
past. The various logical tracts in circulation in the fourteenth

century, despite their great fame and influence at the time, have been little studied in the discussion of meaning in poetry. Treatises on heraldry have been used in the past to find specific examples of colours and devices comparable to those in literature (often with a view towards identifying poetic characters with historical individuals), but the underlying theory about the semiotic relationship between heraldic devices and their owners have never been treated. Works of speculative geometry contain many references to the suitability of geometrical figures as signs of spiritual values, but unless they happen to make specific reference to pentangles, they have gone unused. Finally, there is a large body of doctrinal and homiletic material that either contains explicit statements about the complexity of the relationship between images and their referents or else *exempla* that show signifying connections similar to those in *Sir Gawain and the Green Knight* even when the particular terms may be different. A detailed examination of such works, while focusing on their utility in the interpretation of a few passages in this one poem, should help to extend a great deal the possibilities for understanding both the general problem of symbolism and the particular symbols of individual medieval writers.

1 Pure Signification: The Shield of Truth

A   THE IMPOSITION OF THE SIGN

1   Gawain's Shield

The story-line of *Sir Gawain and the Green Knight* is so full of arresting incidents and surprising turns of events as to set it head and shoulders above all the other Middle English romances. The joyful Christmas celebrations of Arthur and his court are interrupted by the arrival of the monstrous and incongruous Green Knight, and we wonder what he will do next. When he challenges any member of the court to deal him a blow and accept a comparable stroke a year later at his home, we wonder who will accept the challenge. When Gawain steps forward and decapitates the knight, we have no time to feel relief at his success before the knight picks up his head and reminds Gawain of the promise he has made. Even during the intervening year and Gawain's search through the countryside for his appointed rendezvous, the poet's descriptive language focuses the attention of a first-time reader more on the character and the actions than on any possible deeper meaning. While Gawain stays with his genial host Bercilak, we are still led to concentrate on the surface of the action, whether the rapid twistings and turnings of the three hunts or the subtle verbal fencing of the three seduction attempts by Bercilak's wife. Each day, when host and guest meet to exchange their 'winnings,' we focus on the embarrassment we would feel if we were Gawain, or on the suspicions we would feel if we were Bercilak, and on the possibility that somehow the whole genteel scene is going to be broken wide open. Somewhere in the middle of these scenes, although no one seems to be quite sure where, we come to suspect that Bercilak is the Green Knight in disguise, or vice versa, and it takes most of our reading energy to cope with the tone of anticipation and dread of what is to come. Gawain's success in resisting the lady's advances augurs well for his success when he faces up to the Green Knight's axe, and our relief when he is finally spared is only slightly troubled by his continual insistence that he is marked as permanently sinful for accepting, and not exchanging with Bercilak, the lady's magic girdle, in an attempt to preserve his own life.

The story-line, the poet's strong visual imagination and ability to create involving situations, and our own modern predilection for identification with characters and desire to be entertained all combine to give the impression that we need do nothing more than enjoy the poem. It is rare indeed to find a first-time undergraduate reader who sees this as a problem-poem at all. Yet once the classroom discussion has been started, it is far less difficult to provoke the search for deeper meaning here than in many other medieval works. Whether consciously noticed or not, the various passages in which the poet requests interpretation and analysis have been effective.

The belief that such work is required may be raised from the level of intuition to a sounder critical basis by the application of a general medieval principle and by the examination of particular passages in the poem. If the purpose of speech is not only to delight, as does song, but to communicate and to teach, then we ought to be looking at what the poet is trying to teach his audience, not simply at how he intrigues and diverts them. And if the meaning of speech is to be found in the nature of the addressee, then the poem's doctrine must be related to the actual situation of the audience: what point could there be in teaching a fourteenth-century audience how to deal with large green men who do not die when decapitated? The way to demonstrate that the poet did indeed have such concerns is to focus on those passages in the text that do not contribute to the excitement of the plot, that seem incompatible with the desire simply to entertain, and that suggest an interest in moral problems of greater scope than the particular ancient, marvellous situation requires.

There is surely no more obvious such passage in *Sir Gawain and the Green Knight* than the description of the pentangle device on Gawain's shield. As Gawain sets off to find the Green Knight and

keep his bargain to receive a stroke from his axe, the poet suspends
the action for precisely fifty lines to describe the shield and to
explain Gawain's right to carry it:

> Then þay schewed hym þe schelde, þat was of schyr goulez
> Wyth þe pentangel depaynt of pure golde hwez.
> He braydez hit by þe bauderyk, aboute þe hals kestes,
> Þat bisemed þe segge semlyly fayre.
> And quy þe pentangel apendez to þat prynce noble
> I am in tent yow to telle, þof tary hyt me schulde:
> Hit is a syngne þat Salamon set sumquyle
> In bytoknyng of trawþe, bi tytle þat hit habbez,
> For hit is a figure þat haldez fyue poyntez,
> And vche lyne vmbellapez and loukez in oþer,
> And ayquere hit is endelez; and Englych hit callen
> Oueral, as I here, þe endeles knot.
> Forþy hit acordez to þis knyȝt and to his cler armez,
> For ay faythful in fyue and sere fyue syþez
> Gawan watz for gode knawen, and as golde pured,
> Voyded of vche vylany, wyth vertuez ennourned
>   in mote;
>   Forþy þe pentangel nwe
>   He ber in schelde and cote,
>   As tulk of tale most trwe
>   And gentylest knyȝt of lote.
>
> Fyrst he watz funden faultlez in his fyue wyttez,
> And efte fayled neuer þe freke in his fyue fyngres,
> And alle his afyaunce vpon folde watz in þe fyue woundez
> Þat Cryst kaȝt on þe croys, as þe crede tellez;
> And quere-so-euer þys mon in melly watz stad,
> His þro þoȝt watz in þat, þurȝ alle oþer þyngez,
> Þat alle his forsnes he feng at þe fyue joyez
> Þat þe hende heuen-quene had of hir chylde;
> At þis cause þe knyȝt comlyche hade
> In þe inore half of his schelde hir ymage depaynted,
> Þat quen he blusched þerto his belde neuer payred.
> Þe fyft fyue þat I finde þat þe frek vsed
> Watz fraunchyse and felaȝschyp forbe al þyng,
> His clannes and his cortaysye croked were neuer,
> And pité, þat passez alle poyntez, þyse pure fyue

Were harder happed on þat haþel þen on any oþer.
Now alle þese fyue syþez, for soþe, were fetled on þis knyȝt,
And vchone halched in oþer, þat non ende hade,
And fyched vpon fyue poyntez, þat fayld neuer,
Ne samned neuer in no syde, ne sundred nouþer,
Withouten ende at any noke I oquere fynde,
Whereeuer þe gomen bygan, or glod to an ende.
Þerfore on his schene schelde schapen watz þe knot
Ryally wyth red golde vpon red gowlez,
Þat is þe pure pentaungel wyth þe peple called
    with lore.
   Now grayþed is Gawan gay,
   And laȝt his launce ryȝt þore,
   And gef hem alle goud day,
   He wende for euermore. (619–69)[1]

Then they showed him the shield, which was of bright gules, with
the pentangle painted on it in pure gold hues. He takes it by the
baldric and hangs it around his neck, and it suited the knight very
well. And why the pentangle belongs to that noble prince I intend to
tell you, though it delays me. It is a sign that Solomon once established as a token of *trawþ*, which it has a right to be, because it
is a figure that has five points, and each line overlaps and locks into
another, and everywhere it is endless, and the English everywhere, I
hear, call it the endless knot. Therefore it is suited to this knight
and to his bright arms, for, always faithful in five ways and five times
in each way, Gawain was known as good and, like refined gold,
freed of each villainy and adorned with virtues in the field. Therefore
he bore the new pentangle on his shield and coat, as a man most
true of word and the gentlest knight in bearing. First, he was found
faultless in his five senses, and again the man never failed in his
five fingers, and all his trust on earth was in the wounds that Christ
received on the cross, as the creed tells. Wherever this man was
pressed in battle, his firm thought was on this, above all else, that he
received all his courage from the five joys that the gracious queen
of heaven had from her child. For this reason the knight properly had
her image painted on the inside of his shield, so that when he
looked at it his courage never waned. The fifth five that I find that
the knight used was liberality and fellowship above all things;
his cleanness and courtesy were never crooked, and pity, that passes
other qualities – these pure five were more firmly fixed in this

man than in any other. Now all these five multiples, truly, were
fastened together in this knight, and each one was joined into
another, so that it had no end, and fixed upon five points that never
failed, nor came together in any side or separated either, without
end at any angle anywhere, I find, wherever the *gomen* began or came
to an end. Therefore on his bright shield this knot was fashioned,
royally with red gold upon red gules, that is called the pure pentangle
by people with learning. Now Gawain is made ready, and he took
his lance right there; he bade them all good day, he thought for
evermore.

The sheer bulk of this passage is a clear indication even to a casual
reader that the poet wishes his words here to be read very closely: a
fifty-line description of the arming of a knight who is departing to
keep an appointment for an unarmed encounter suggests rather
strongly that a naturalistic reading is insufficient. The poet's use of
the pentangle as a device could not help but attract critical interest
and provoke comparisons with other symbolic pentangles, since the
form belongs to many different systems of symbolism throughout
the world, beginning with the Pythagoreans. What should prevent,
however, or at least delay, the recourse to alien systems of interpretation is the fact that the pentangle is called a 'sign' and that the
information contained in its description is precisely what we would
expect the poet to provide if he wished his pentangle to be understood in the context of his own society's sign theory. The correlation
of the poet's data with the logician's theory is the first step required
for an interpretation of the passage.

2   Natural and *ad placitum* Signification

The definitions of *res* and *signum* quoted from Augustine above,
sufficient for their original purposes, provide only the barest starting-
point for an understanding of the complexities of signification as
studied in even the initial stages of education in logic in the fourteenth century. Students were called upon to learn standard explanations of the way in which a particular thing comes to be a sign, of
the manner in which we know what it signifies, and of the nature of
the relationship between a sign and its referent. Even in the area
of lexical semantics there is much to be learned from the theoretical
works current in the *Gawain* poet's age.

A fourteenth-century student would first encounter a formal

system concerned with the connections of signs to referents in an introductory course in logic. The standard text for such a course, throughout our period and for many years afterwards, was Aristotle's *Peri Hermeneias* (*On Interpretation*).[2] This work begins with what Aristotle believed was the most basic matter of the topic, but the fourteenth-century student was expected to start a level deeper. While Aristotle was content to begin with definitions of *noun, verb, negation, affirmation, statement,* and *sentence,* the terminist logicians such as Peter of Spain move by a process of reasoning to *sound* as the true ground of their study:

> quia disputatio non potest haberi nisi mediante sermone, nec sermo nisi mediante voce, omnis autem vox est sonus, – ideo a sono tamquam a priori inchoandum est.[3]

> since there can be no disputation without the mediation of speech and no speech without the mediation of voice, and all voice is sound, – therefore we must begin with sound as the beginning.

From this starting-point these logicians move by division to the real subject-matter of their investigations. Sound is subdivided into two categories, the vocal (for example, utterances) and the non-vocal (for example, footsteps); utterances are then divided into the significant and the non-significant, the usual example of the latter being the nonsense words *buba blictrix*. Finally, significant utterances are divided into those that signify naturally (*naturaliter*) and those that have their meaning by convention (*ad placitum*). There is an impressive sameness about the ways in which the various treatises present this distinction and the examples they use, not, it would seem, because of dependence of one on another but because they are all expressions of a long-standing tradition:

> Vocum significativarum alia significativa ad placitum, alia naturaliter. Vox significativa naturaliter est illa que apud omnes idem representat, ut gemitus infirmorum, latratus canum. Vox significativa ad placitum est illa que ad voluntatem instituentis aliquid representat, ut *homo*.[4]

> Some significant utterances signify by convention, others naturally. The naturally significant utterance is that which represents the same thing among all people, such as the moaning of the sick and

the barking of dogs. The conventionally significant utterance is that which represents something by the will of the institutor, such as *homo*.

Illa dicitur significativa naturaliter que aliquid significat a natura, ut gemitus infirmorum, latratus canum ... Vox significativa ad placitum est illa que ad voluntatem instituentis aliquid significat.[5]

That utterance is called naturally significant which signifies something by nature, such as the moaning of the sick and the barking of dogs ... The conventionally significant utterance is that which signifies something by the will of the institutor.

Naturaliter, que natura agente aliquid significat, ut gemitus infirmorum et similia. Ad placitum, que ex humana institutione significationem recepit.[6]

The kind that signifies naturally is the kind produced by nature and significant of something, such as the groans of the sick; the kind that signifies by convention is the kind that acquires its signification as the result of some human custom.[7]

The ground for this claim that the basic elements of human language are established by convention and not through nature is the obvious fact that words are not the same among all people. Aristotle compares the diversity of words to the diversity of alphabets in a passage that Aquinas, in his commentary on the *Peri Hermeneias*, explains as follows:

Voces autem naturaliter formantur; unde et apud quosdam dubitatum fuit, utrum naturaliter significent. Sed Aristoteles hic determinat ex similitudine litterarum, quae sicut non sunt eaedem apud omnes, ita nec voces. Unde manifeste relinquitur quod sicut nec litterae, ita nec voces naturaliter significant, sed ex institutione humana.[8]

Since utterances are naturally formed, some have wondered whether they signify naturally. But Aristotle decides the matter here by a comparison to letters. They are not the same among all people, nor are utterances. Whence it clearly follows that just as letters do not signify naturally, so neither do utterances, but rather through human institution.

The commentators point out not only the obvious fact that different things are given different names by different nations, but also that there are variations within one group over a period of time, as Ammonius says:

> composuerant enim ad invicem Hellenes quidem his nominibus has res vocare, Indi autem aliis et Aegyptii aliis, et iidem eadem aliquando quidem aliis, aliquando vero aliis.[9]

> For the Greeks had agreed to call certain things by certain names, the Indians by other names, and the Egyptians by still others, and the same people call the same things by some names at one time and by others at another time.

In a more widely known work, Augustine makes the same point, including specific examples (one of which continues to trouble elementary students studying both Latin and Greek) to reinforce the general point about the conventionality of signs:

> beta uno eodemque sono apud Graecos litterae, apud Latinos holeris nomen est; et cum dico 'lege,' in his duabus syllabis aliud Graecus, aliud Latinus intellegit – sicut ergo hae omnes significationes pro suae cuiusque socieatatis consensione animos mouent et, quia diuersa consensio est, diuerse mouent, nec ideo consenserunt in eas homines, quia iam ualebant ad significationem, sed ideo ualent, quia consenserunt in eas.[10]

> And the single sign *beta* means a letter among the Greeks but a vegetable among the Latins. When I say *lege*, a Greek understands one thing by these two syllables, a Latin understands another. Therefore, just as all of these significations move men's minds in accordance with the consent of their societies, and because this consent varies, they move them differently, nor do men agree upon them because of an innate value, but they have a value because they are agreed upon.[11]

This same awareness of the conventionality of language and interest in the difference between various group of speakers may be seen also in popular vernacular literature. Chaucer, for example, points out in *Troilus and Criseyde* that words change over time, and incidentally moves by analogy to the larger case of human social behaviour:

> Ye knowe ek that in forme of speche is chaunge
> Withinne a thousand yeer, and wordes tho
> That hadden pris, now wonder nyce and straunge
> Us thinketh hem, and yet thei spake hem so,
> And spedde as wel in love as men now do;
> Ek for to wynnen love in sondry ages,
> In sondry londes, sondry ben usages.[12]

> You know also that there is change in the form of speech within a thousand years, and words that then were valued now seem very strange to us, and yet they spoke them that way, and fared as well in love as men do now; similarly, for winning love, in different ages and different lands there are different methods.

For all these writers, then, the separate elements of language, the items of vocabulary, have their basic meaning because of human institution and preserve it over time within a particular language-group only by reason of general convention and agreement.

While modern critics generally make a strong division between language theory and the theory of interpretation of visible signs, medieval sign theorists considered their chosen field of study to include all manner of things that signify. Signs are divided into categories not on the basis of the material out of which they are made but according to their manner of signifying. Augustine excludes smoke, animal tracks, and sad faces from his discussion not because they are not signs but because they do not signify by intention.[13] When all the conditions are met, it is possible to discuss written words, hieroglyphics, gestures, and so on according to the same general distinctions and rules that are applied to spoken words.[14]

Such is the case with the pentangle as described in *Sir Gawain and the Green Knight*. It is a sign for *trawþ*, that is, for *trawþ* itself, not for the word *trawþ*. Further, it is a conventional sign, and not a natural one, for if it were a natural sign, according to contemporary theory, it would have the same meaning for all people at all times and would certainly not need the lengthy explanation it is given. It would also not need an institutor, yet the poet tells us that it became a sign for *trawþ* at a particular point in time as the result of the action of a particular person: 'Hit is a syngne þat Salamon set sumquyle' (625). It therefore fits the definition of a *signum ad placitum* well enough to allow profitable analysis along the lines drawn by the terminist logicians.

In addition to being a sign for *trawþ*, the pentangle is also a visible object, a *res* that must have a name of its own, a sign to refer to it. In this case, however, there are two different verbal signs for the same referent. It is called the 'pentaungel' by people with learning (664), and it is called 'þe endeles knot' by the general run of Englishmen (629–30). This doubling of the sign is not an indication of confusion or a cause for concern, however, as it leads us to some of the most interesting evidence concerning the possibilities for learning about an object through analysis of the signs imposed on it.

3   Imposition according to Qualities

From an Aristotelian perspective the most serious objection to the belief that the signifying relationship is arbitrary is the empirical fact that language is considerably more stable than most other institutions not grounded in nature. Political practices, artistic techniques, musical taste, and other such cultural elements of life are demonstrably subject to change over short periods of time, whereas the relationship between words and their referents changes slowly, or piecemeal. In the event of a rapid or extreme change we have the feeling that something that should be permanent has been undermined or perverted. The man who would make signs mean whatever he wants them to mean provokes either laughter, like Humpty Dumpty, or bitter scorn, like the anonymous heraldic theorist in *Gargantua* who, on his own authority, declares that white stands for faith.[15]

This objection is faced by Lambert of Auxerre, who brings added precision to the meaning of the word *voluntas* to overcome the problem:

> Vox significativa ad placitum est illa que ad voluntatem institutentis aliquid significat. Sed contra dicit Aristoteles in secundo *Physicorum* quod duo sunt principia rerum, scilicet natura et voluntas. Natura est principium intransmutabile: natura enim non assuescit in contrarium. Quod patet in igne cui inest caliditas per naturam, ita quod frigiditas non potest ei inesse. Voluntas autem est principium transmutabile, unde se habet ad oppositum; quod patet, quia homo qui est agens a voluntate potest sedere et non sedere, si voluerit. Si ergo

a voluntate instituentis esset significatum dictionis, transmutari
posset illud significatum, quod falsum est. Ad hoc dicendum est quod
de voluntate est loqui dupliciter. Uno modo prout est libera et de
tali verum est quod est principium transmutabile; vel possumus loqui
de voluntate prout est recta ratione considerata, vel per rationem
abstracta, et sic voluntas non est principium transmutabile, et hoc
modo voluntas est principium imponendi voces ad significandum, et
non primo modo.[16]

A conventionally signifying utterance is that which signifies something by the will of the institutor. Aristotle, however, says in the
second book of the *Physics* that there are two principles of things,
namely, nature and will. Nature is the unchanging principle, for
nature does not admit contraries. This is clear in fire: heat inheres in
it by nature, so that coldness cannot be in it. Now will is the
changeable principle, whence it admits opposites. This is clear, in that
a man who is acting by will is able to sit and not to sit, according
to his will. If therefore the meaning of a word were from the will of
the institutor, that meaning could be changed. But this is not so.
In answer to this objection we must say that there are two ways to
talk about will. In the first way we may speak of it in so far as it
is free, and it is true in such a way that it is a changeable principle.
But we may also speak about will in so far as it is considered by
right reason or derived through reason, and thus will is not a changeable principle. In this way, and not in the first way, will is the
principle of imposing utterances for the purpose of signifying.

According to this view, human language is stable in spite of its
conventional basis because the signifying relationships have been
established properly, that is, by right reason. When we are asked to
consider the special case of a sign that has a known first institutor,
we may know that the sign will be stable if he has made use of
recta ratio. His lead will be followed, and the sign he imposes will
acquire the added authority of common usage in a particular group
over a long period of time.

The words in which the traces of right reasoning are most evident
are those for which we can find meaningful etymologies. It would
be impossible for a medieval writer not to be aware of the belief that
hundreds of Latin words are derived from other words, in Latin,
Greek, or Hebrew, which indicate their essential meaning or direct
our attention to some important fact about their referents. It is

not surprising that Lambert, when he wishes to cite examples to show the operation of right reason in the creation of signs, chooses two common Isidorean etymologies:

> Nam ut in pluribus voces imponuntur ad significandas res secundum rerum proprietates et etiam secundum rationem ut homo dicitur, quia est factus de humo, et lapis quasi ledens pedem et sic de aliis.[17]

> For in many cases utterances are imposed to signify things according to the properties of the things and also according to reason, as man is called 'homo' since he was made from earth (*de humo*) and a stone is called 'lapis' as it harms the foot (*ledens pedem*), and so forth.

This belief, derived ultimately from Plato's *Cratylus*, that certain signs are related to the properties of the objects they signify, constitutes the second argument against the *ad placitum* theory of meaning. Its origin in Platonic discussions did not mean, however, that it was ignored or dismissed out of hand by the medieval commentators on Aristotle, in part because their Greek sources included Neoplatonists such as Ammonius. Though it is clear that the word *homo* is not in any sense a natural sign in Aristotelian terms, since it is not universal and since it is derived from the conventionally imposed word *humus* and not from the material object signified by that word, still the views ascribed to Plato are treated fairly. Aquinas considers not only the main argument of the naturalist position but also treats its response to the empiricist objection that if signs are natural, there would not be two signs for one referent:

> *Quidam* vero dixerunt quod nomina non naturaliter significant quantum ad hoc, quod eorum significatio non est a natura, ut Aristoteles hic intendit; quantum vero ad hoc naturaliter significant quod eorum significatio congruit naturis rerum, ut Plato dixit. Nec obstat quod una res multis nominibus significatur: quia unius rei possunt esse multae similitudines; et similiter ex diversis proprietatibus possunt uni rei multa diversa nomina imponi.[18]

> Some, however, have said that although nouns do not signify naturally in so far as their signification is not from nature, as Aristotle says here, still they do signify naturally in so far as their signification accords with the natures of the things, as Plato said. Nor is it any impediment that one thing is signified by many names, for there can

be many copies of one thing, and similarly many diverse names
can be imposed on one thing in accordance with diverse properties.

Ammonius provides an example of such an situation in his commentary on the *Peri Hermeneias*. There are three different Greek
words for *man* in more or less current usage, for which he provides
three (fanciful) etymological explanations;

> hoc nomen anthropos et merops et brotos significat idem, scilicet
> hominem, sed hoc quidem scilicet anthropos secundum quod sursum
> aspicit, hoc autem scilicet merops secundum quod partabilem habet
> vitam, hoc autem scilicet brotos secundum casum animae in
> generatione.[19]

> *Anthropos* and *merops* and *brotos* signify the same thing, namely
> 'man.' [He is called] anthropos according to the fact that he looks
> upward, merops in that he has a life divisible into parts, and brotos
> because of the fall of the soul in generation.

This situation parallels the two different names attributed to the
device on Gawain's shield. These names, each sanctioned by the
usage of a particular group, are both derived from its essential qualities. The people 'with lore' know that it is a 'pentangle' and would
recognize that its name accords with its five sides and five points.
The student of grammar would know by heart the verse from Eberhard of Bethune's *Graecismus*, 'Est penta quinque, pentaptota dicitur
inde'; 'Penta is five, from which we get the word *pentaptote* [a
word that has five cases].'[20] Students of mathematics would know
the sequence beginning with the triangle and proceeding to 'Alia
quattuor et vocatur quadratum. Alia vero quinque et vocatur penta-
gonus et sic in infinitum'; 'Another figure has four sides and is
called a quadrilateral. Yet another has five sides, and is called a
pentagon, and so on to infinity.'[21] Anyone with the beginnings
of clerical learning, or one who paid attention to sermons, would
recognize the connection from the etymology of Pentecost: 'Pentecoste dicitur a penta, quod est quinque, et costes, quod est decem, et
dicitur Pentecoste quinquagesimus dies a Pascha'; 'Pentecost is
derived from *penta*, which is five, and *costes*, which is ten, and the
fiftieth day after Easter is called Pentecost.'[22]
The common English name for the device, like the learned name,
is related to the properties of the object it designates. It is called

the 'endless knot' because there is no point at which it comes to an
end, as we are repeatedly told (629, 657, 660, 661). The endlessness
of the device itself is the quality, then, that decides the name it
is most generally given. There are two names because the object has
diverse properties, and both names are stable because they have
been imposed according to right reason.

These names are related to their referent in a manner parallel to
the way in which the pentangle itself is related to its referent, *trawþ*.
We are told that it is a 'syngne ... set ... / In bytoknyng of trawþe,
bi tytle þat hit habbez' (625–6), which means, in this context, that it
is chosen as a sign for *trawþ* because it relates to some essential
quality or qualities of *trawþ* itself. The poet seems to be saying that,
just as the name 'endless knot' and the name 'pentangle' are imposed on the pentangle as signs relating to its endlessness and its
five-foldness, so too the pentangle is imposed on *trawþ* as a sign
because *trawþ* is both endless and fivefold. Solomon performed his
task according to right reason, placing in front of us a visible sign
whose properties may be examined and analysed in order to learn
about an invisible quality.

B   ENDLESS SIGNS IN THE POET'S TRADITION

The eager search for symbolic pentangles in the poet's culture (and
indeed, in many other cultures) has distracted attention from a large
number of symbolic endless figures, often meticulously glossed,
that are of great assistance in determining the nature of the general
field in which the poet was operating.[23] One of the most common
of these images is the circle. In *Pearl*, to begin with an obvious
example, we are told that the endless roundness is what makes a
pearl the appropriate symbol for the kingdom of heaven:

> This makellez perle þat bozt is dere
> Þe joueler gef for alle hys god
> Is lyke þe reme of heuenesse clere
> So sayde þe fader of folde & flode
> For hit is wemlez clene & clere
> & endelez rounde & blyþe of mode
> & commune to alle þat ryztwys were.   (733–9)[24]

The jeweller gave all his goods in exchange for this matchless pearl,
that is dear bought. It is like the clear kingdom of heaven, so said

the father of land and sea. For it is spotless, pure, and clear, and endlessly round, and serene in mood, and belonging equally to all that
were righteous.

The pearl is also used as a sign in *Purity*, but with somewhat different referents. Here it is compared first with Christ, whose purity
we should imitate ('Þenne confourme þe to Kryst & þe clene make /
Þat euer is polyced als playn as þe perle seluen' 1067–8; 'Then
make yourself like Christ, and make yourself pure, for he is polished
as smooth as the pearl itself') and then to the soul in a state of
grace ('Þou may schyne þurȝ schryfte þaȝ þou haf schome serued / &
pure þe with penaunce til þou a perle worþe' 1115–16; 'You may
shine through confession, though you have served shame, and clean
yourself with penance until you become a pearl'); here too, roundness is one of the essential characteristics mentioned (1121).

The author of *Dives and Pauper* connects roundness and endlessness in his explanation of the use of a ring at weddings. After a
scientific explanation of the fact that it is placed on the fourth finger
(there is a vein connecting that finger directly to the heart) and a
moral explanation of the fact that the husband gives his wife only
one ring ('in tokene þat þay schuldyn louyn hem togedere synguler-
lyche'; 'as a sign that they should love each other exclusively'),
he proceeds to a symbolic explanation of the ring itself: 'The ryng is
round aboute & hath non ende in tokene þat her loue schulde ben
endeles & noþing departyn hem but deth alone';[25] 'The ring is round
and has no end as a sign that their love should be endless and
nothing should separate them but death alone.'

John Mirk, in his *Sermo de Nupcijs*, provides a similar explanation,
but one that is more orthodox in its attitude towards married love:

> Þerfore þe prest blessuth a ring, þat betokeneth God, þat hath neyther
> begynnyng ne endyng, and duth hit on hur fyngur þat haþe a veyne
> to hure herte, tokenyng þat he schal loue God oure all thyng, and
> þanne hure husbond.[26]

> Therefore the priest blesses a ring, which signifies God, that has
> neither beginning nor end, and puts it on the finger that has a vein
> leading to her heart, as a sign that she shall love God above all
> things, and then her husband.

Another such image may be found in the explanation in a fourteenth-
century sermon of the woman wearing a crown of twelve stars in

Revelation 12:1. For this preacher the crown is a unified whole but nevertheless composed of twelve separable parts and therefore comparable to the unified yet composite pentangle:

> Vppon þis glorious Virgyns hede þer was a crowne of xij sterres, by
> þe wiche crowne may be vndirstond þe perfeccion of all vertewes. A
> crowne is rounde in figure. Hit is set to þe hed, and be-clippeþ it
> in euery parte. Euen so þe bounde of vertewes is rounde, havyng non
> ende, but strecheþ to eternite, bryngynge þe soule to perpetuall
> blis. Be þise sterres beþ vertewes vndirstond. And like as þe sterres
> have þe liȝthe of þe sonne, vt dicit Philosophus in libro De Proprieta-
> tibus Elementorum, so all vertewes haue þer liȝthe of þe sonne of
> grace, for withowte grace, propurly to speke, þer is no morall vertewe.
> Þis crowne shyned excellently in þe hede of þis glorious Ladie, for
> þis was plente of all vertewes, where-by wicked spirites were put in
> gret drede and she wondir amyable to God and to all angels: 'Vna
> est columba mea, perfecta mea,' Cantici 6.
>   Þise xij sterres oþur xij vertewes Seynt Poule reherseþ, ad Galatas,
> 5ᵗᵒ, seing þus, 'Fructus Spiritus est caritas, gaudium, pax, paciencia,
> longanimitas, bonitas, benignitas, mansuetudo, fides, modestia,
> continencia, castitas.'[27]

On this glorious Virgin's head there was a crown of twelve stars, by which may be understood the perfection of all virtues. A crown is a round figure. It is set upon the head, and surrounds it on all sides. Even so, the boundary of virtues is round, and has no end, but stretches to eternity, bringing the soul to perpetual bliss. By these stars virtues are understood. Just as the stars have their light from the sun, as the Philosopher says in the book *On the Properties of Elements*, so all virtues have their light from the sun of grace, for without grace, to speak properly, there is no moral virtue. This crown shone excellently on the head of this glorious lady, for there was a sufficiency of virtues, whereby wicked spirits were put into dread and she was wondrously lovable to God and to all angels: 'One is my dove, my perfect one is but one,' Canticles 6:8.

These twelve stars or twelve virtues are listed by St Paul, in Galatians 5, as he says, 'But the fruit of the Spirit is charity, joy, peace, patience, benignity, goodness, longanimity, mildness, faith, modesty, continency, chastity.'

Gawain's pentangle device, then, is part of a more general phenomenon of physically endless objects signifying a temporally endless

quality. In addition, however, it is more insistently *geometrical*.
The simple unity of the circle requires little explanation, and there
is no difficulty in making a circle a unified yet composite figure
by setting symbolic gemstones around its perimeter. The *Gawain*
poet's desire to present a more complex idea to his audience results
in a more complex sign to convey it.

Strictly speaking, any plane geometrical figure could be considered
endless. The circle is generally given pride of place because of its
regularity and the fact that it lacks even corners to be considered as
beginning or ending points. But given the fact that the poet wanted
a figure that would be truly composite in addition to being endless,
there are many properties in the pentangle that make it especially
appropriate. Five is in a special category according to medieval
number theory, in that it is a so-called circular number, which re-
produces itself in its last digit when raised to its powers. This
property is discussed at length in the standard fourteenth-century
mathematics text, the *De Arithmetica* of Boethius:

> Nam quinquies quinque, qui fit 25, ab 5 progressus, in eosdem 5
> desinit. Et si hos rursum quinquies ducas, in eosdem 5 eorum termi-
> nus veniet. Quinquies 25 fiunt 125, et si hoc rursus quinquies
> ducas, in quinarium numerum extremitas terminabitur. Atque hoc
> usque in infinitum idem semper evenit.[28]

> For 5 times 5, which makes 25, starts from 5 and ends in the same
> number, 5. And if you multiply that by 5 again, the end turns out to
> be 5 again. For 5 times 25 makes 125, and if you multiply by 5
> again, the answer will end with the number 5. And this always hap-
> pens up to infinity.

Since six, the only other circular number, would yield a disunified
Star of David composed of two superimposed triangles, five is the
best arithmetical choice for a composite unified figure.

The pentangle is connected with an idea of endless self-replication
in a geometrical as well as an arithmetical fashion. Every regular
pentangle contains within itself a regular pentagon, in which a new,
similar pentangle may be inscribed. This process may be repeated
forever with decreasing pentangles. Secondly, each side of a pentangle
bisects each line it crosses into two unequal segments such that
the ratio of the whole line to the larger segment is the same as the
ratio of the larger segment to the smaller segment. This proportion is

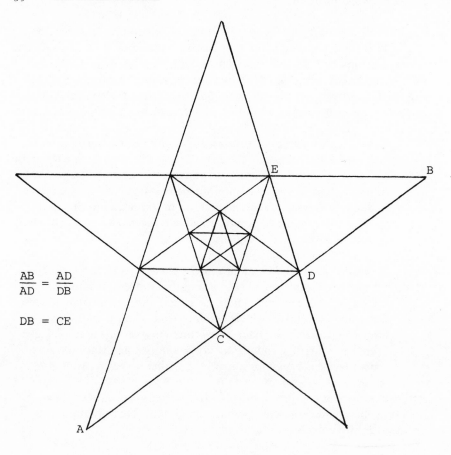

$$\frac{AB}{AD} = \frac{AD}{DB}$$

$$DB = CE$$

Figure 1 The Geometers' Pentangle

the so-called golden section: the two segments are the length and
breadth of the self-replicating golden rectangle. The smaller of the
two segments is equal to the side of the inscribed smaller pentangle,
which is further dissected according to the same ratio. The result
is that each line or segment stands in the same relationship to the
next smaller line.[29] (See Figure 1.) From both an arithmetic and a
geometrical point of view the pentangle is a figure that keeps coming
back to where it started, 'usque in infinitum.'

For a pure mathematician, however, it is not proper to speak of
such a thing as an infinite figure. The process of self-replication

might well be endlessly repeatable, but the resultant figure is not ·
spatially infinite. Speculation about infinite geometry leads to logical
contradictions that for the mathematician, at least, invalidate the
whole argument. Nicholas Oresme, for example, examines the question of the infinite circle in his *Quaestiones super Geometriam
Euclidis* and offers first a common-sense argument for its existence:

> Consequentur queritur: *Utrum secundum ymaginacionem mathe-
> maticam debeat concedi, quod sit aliquis circulus infinitus ita, quod
> ex hoc non sequitur contradictio.* Et arguitur quod sic; quia, si
> sumatur aliquis circulus et in prima parte proporcionali hore crescat
> in duplo et in secunda in triplo et sic in infinitum, in fine ille
> circulus esset infinitus; et huiusmodi antecedens non repugnat yma-
> ginacioni, igitur nec consequens.[30]

> It is asked whether *secundum imaginationem mathematicam* an
> infinite circle can exist in such a way that it does not lead to a con-
> tradiction. The question is first answered in the affirmative. Indeed,
> if a circle were taken which became twice as great in the first
> proportional part of an hour, three times as great in the second, etc.,
> *in inf.*, this circle would ultimately be infinite, and since the ante-
> cedent is not *contra imaginationem*, neither is the consequent.[31]

After considering the problem from five different points of view,
however, he decides on the opposing argument, that such a circle is
an impossibility on logical grounds:

> Oppositum arguitur quia, si esset circulus, esset figura et esset suo
> termino clausa, et sic non esset infinita sed finita.[32]

> The opposite is argued: if it were a circle, it would be a figure, and
> since a figure is contained by its boundary or boundaries (Euclid
> I, *Def.* 14), it would be not infinite but finite.[33]

In the purely mathematical tradition, then, it is clear that 'figure'
and 'infinite' are considered to be mutually exclusive. While it is
not thereby made impossible to describe such a figure, as we shall
see, we cannot draw one, nor could the poet expect us to believe
that one could be drawn on a shield. In his desire to create for Gawain a heraldic sign that is comparable to an infinite figure, he must
choose one whose perimeter is endless even though its enclosed

area is finite. Further, by using this figure as a *signum*, he has created the perfect linguistic *coincidentia oppositorum*, an interminable term.

The infinite circle is a contradiction in terms, and infinite geometry leads its practitioners into areas where apparently firm definitions blur. But such logical problems proved to be no impediment to the practice, so productive were the results for speculations about the infinite. Bartholomaeus Anglicus, in his influential *De Proprietatibus Rerum*, is only one of many medieval writers who are quite prepared to discuss and interpret the 'sphaera intellectualis, cuius centrum vbique est, circumferentia vero nusquam,'[34] that is, a 'spere intellectual of þe which þe centrum, þat is þe myddel poynt, is in eueriche place and þe roundenes nowhere in no place.'[35] A brief discussion and a lengthy bibliography concerning this topos may be found in Curtius.[36]

Perhaps the fullest use of this kind of material was made by Nicholas of Cusa, who summed up the whole of the pre-existing tradition of infinite geometry. He asserts that the endlessness of various infinite geometrical figures renders them all identical but, far from abandoning speculation about them because of the consequent loss of distinctness, considers them all the more apt to his purposes:

> Dico igitur si esset linea infinita, illa esset recta, illa esset triangulus, illa esset circulus et esset sphaera; et pariformiter, si esset sphaera infinita, illa esset circulus, triangulus, et linea; et ita de triangulo infinito atque circulo infinito idem dicendum est.[37]

> If there were an infinite line, I maintain that it would be at once a straight line, a triangle, a circle, a sphere; similarly, if there were an infinite sphere, it would at once be a circle, a triangle and a line; and it would be likewise with the infinite triangle and infinite circle.[38]

Some of the proofs he presents for these equivalences are rather suspect, in that they depend on the indeterminacy of the word 'infinite,' but others seem to proceed according to acceptable geometrical reasoning. As an example of the first group of proofs the demonstration that the infinite triangle is the infinite circle will suffice:

> Nam sit triangulus ABC causatus per positionem, per circumducti-

onem lineae AB, quousque B venit in C, A fixo remanente: Non habet
dubium, quando linea AB esset infinita et penitus circumduceretur
B, quousque rediret ad initium, circulum maximum causari, cuius BC
est portio. Et quia est portio arcus infiniti, tunc est linea recta BC.
Et quoniam omnis pars infiniti est infinita, igitur BC non est minor
integro arcu circumferentiae infinitae. Erit igitur BC non tantum
portio sed completissima circumferentia. Quare necessarium est
triangulum ABC esse circulum maximum.[39]

Let us suppose that the triangle A-B-C is described by the line A-B
moving from the fixed point A until it falls on C; were the line infinite
and were it to continue till it returned to its initial position, there
is no doubt we would have the infinite circle of which B-C is a part.
Being a part of an infinite arc, B-C is then a straight line. Now as
every part of the infinite is infinite, therefore B-C is not smaller than
the entire, infinite circumference; B-C, therefore, is not only a part,
but is, in the fullest sense, the circumference. Necessarily we must
conclude that the triangle A-B-C is the infinite circle.[40] (See Figure 2.)

The proof that the circumference of the infinite circle is a straight
line, an apparently more difficult undertaking, is, in contrast, handled
quite persuasively:

> si igitur curva linea in sua curvitate recipit minus, quanto circumfer-
> entia fuerit maioris circuli, igitur circumferentia maximi circuli,
> quae maior esse non potest, est minima curva; quare maxima recta.
> Concidit igitur cum maximo minimum, ita ut ad oculum videatur
> necessarium esse, quod maxima linea sit recta maxime et minime
> curva. Nec hic potest remanere scrupulus dubii, quando in figura
> hic lateraliter videtur, quomodo arcus CD maioris circuli plus recedit
> a curvitate quam arcus EF minoris circuli, et ille plus a curvitate
> recedit quam arcus GH adhuc minoris circuli; quare linea recta AB erit
> arcus maximi circuli, qui maior esse non potest.[41]

Now if the curve of the circumference becomes less curved as the
circle expands, the circumference of the greatest possible circle will
be the smallest possible curve; it will, therefore, be absolutely
straight. The maximum and minimum are, therefore, so identified
that we most clearly perceive that in the infinite there is the absolute
maximum of straightness with the absolute minimum of curve. A

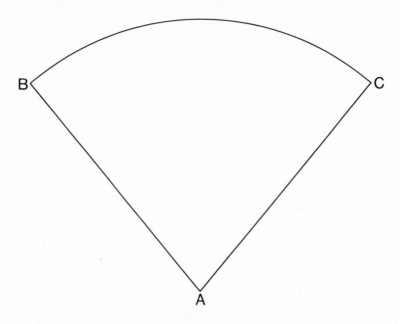

Figure 2 The infinite triangle is the infinite circle

study of the figure here given will dispel all possible doubt on this
point. We see that the arc C-D of the larger circle is less curved
than the arc E-F of the smaller circle, and that E-F is itself less curved
than the arc G-H of a still smaller circle; the straight line A-B will,
therefore, be the arc of the greatest possible circle.[42] (See Figure 3.)

In each of these cases the writer is in no way troubled by the
fact that his concern with endless figures involves him in apparent
logical contradictions, but seems rather to relish the fact that opposites are reunited and definitional boundaries vanish.

These endless objects and figures give us a general view of the
semantic context activated by the poet for his audience by the use of
the endless knot, but the statement he is making within that tradition is rather more complex. It is not enough to recognize that he
has constructed an object like the ring, the crown, and the infinite
circle, since the awareness of that object as a *res* is only the first
step towards understanding its meaning.

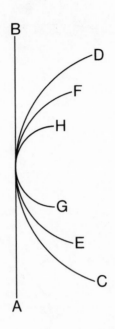

Figure 3 The infinite circle is a straight line

C   THE REFERENT OF THE ENDLESS SIGN

I   Examples from the Tradition

The infinite geometrical figures discussed above differ from figures
acceptable to pure mathematicians such as Oresme in that, as
res, they are self-contradictory; they are also different in that they
are always used as *signa*. When Bartholomaeus Anglicus presents his
description of the infinite sphere, he says that it is a sign for God,
and he includes the name of an ancient wise man as its first institutor and an explanation of his *ratio*; in short, he provides all the
elements included by the *Gawain* poet in his presentation of the
pentangle:

> ipse solus imcomprehensibilis est & interminabilis, & a nullo prae-
> terquam a semetipso cognitus. Nam ipse solus sui ipsius contempla-
> tor maximus est, vnde ad eius totalem comprehensionem nulla

potest pertingere creatura cum sit infinitus in se, virtute tamen sua
infinita finit & terminat vniversa propter quod termegistus describens
Deum prout potuit: ait sic, Deus est sphaera intellectualis, cuius
centrum vbique est, circumferentia vero nusquam. Divina essentia in
se considerata perfecta est ad modum sphaerae, quia non habet
principium neque finem, sed prout consideratur vt eam deducens res
inesse & eam limitans & finiens, sic dicitur esse centrum, quia
sicut centrum finit lineas & ab ipso lineae deducuntur, ita Deus
deducit creaturas & limitat & finit eas.[43]

He allone is incomprehensibil and may not be biclipped, noþir is
iknowe at fulle but of hymself allone, for he allone is heiest and most
parfit in contemplacioun. Þerfore no creature may reche to compre-
hende hym atte fulle. Þeiȝ he be hendeles in hymself, ȝit by hys
endeles vertue he endeþ and ordeyneth ende and termes to alle þinges.
Þerfore Trymegistus descriueth as he may and seiþ in þis manere:
God is a spere intellectual of þe which þe centrum, þat is þe myddell
poynt, is in eueriche place and þe roundenes nowhere in no place.
Þe *essencia* of God in hitsilf iknowe is parfit in þe manere of a
spere, and þe lynes beþ idrawe þerfrom; so God ledeþ creatures and
lettiþ hem in meres and endes and merkes and boundes.[44]

The ubiquity of this sign shows that Hermes Trismegistus performed
his task as first institutor in accordance with *recta ratio*, as the
qualities of the *signum* correspond to the qualities of the referent:
both the intellectual sphere and God are endless, and just as the
undefined centre defines the rest of the sphere, so too a limitless
God imposes limits on all of creation.

In like manner Nicholas of Cusa's purpose in leading his readers
through extensive passages of geometrical reasoning was to establish
the figures so created as signs; not surprisingly, he sees an exact
correspondence between the infinite triangle and the Trinity:

Et ista clare in nostro exemplo videntur, ubi simplicissima linea est
triangulus et e converso simplex triangulus est unitas linealis. Hic
etiam videtur, quomodo numerari anguli trianguli per unum, duo, tria
non possunt, cum quilibet sit in quolibet – ut ait Filius: 'Ego in
Patre et Pater in me.' Iterum, veritas trianguli requirit tres angulos.
Sunt igitur hic verissime tres anguli, et unusquisque maximus, et
omnes unum maximum. Requirit insuper veritas trianguli, quod unus

angulus not sit alius; et ita hic requirit veritas unitatis simplicissi-
mae essentiae, quod tres illi anguli non sint aliqua tria distincta,
sed unum. Et hoc etiam verum est hic.[45]

All this is made evident by our example, in which the infinitely
simple line is a triangle and conversely the infinite triangle is one
line. It is also clear from this that the angles of the triangle cannot be
numbered 1, 2, and 3, since they are all identified with one another:
'The Father is in Me and I in the Father,' as the Son says. In addition,
a true triangle must have three angles; most certainly, then, there
are three angles here, and each is infinite and all are one infinite.
Moreover, the nature of a triangle demands that the angles should be
distinct; here the nature of the infinite oneness of essence demands
that these three angles be not really distinct but one angle. This
is also verified here.[46]

The possibilities of relating mathematical thought to particular
philosophical and theological truths did not go unnoticed among the
pure mathematicians. Thomas Bradwardine, better known for his
theological works and his studies on velocity, wrote a *Geometria
Speculativa* that displays his

concern with relating the mathematics being expounded to philosophy, even to selecting his mathematical material on the basis of
its potential philosophical relevance. Such a guiding principle was
surely in Bradwardine's mind when he saw fit to have his compen-
dium treat of such philosophically pregnant matters as the horn angle,
the incommensurability of the diagonal of a square, and the puzzle
of the possible inequality of infinities.[47]

Similarly, the endless physical objects discussed previously are of
interest to the writers not simply as *res* but as *signa* of endless, invisible substances. For John Mirk the wedding ring is endlessly
round as a sign for God's endlessness. For the *Gawain* poet, in *Pearl*
and *Purity*, the roundness of the pearl is an indication of the endless
purity of Christ or the endless bliss of the kingdom of heaven. For
the writer of the sermon about the Virgin, the roundness of her
crown is a sign of her eternal blessedness.

That the referents for these signs are all divine or associated with
divinity is in no way accidental. In fact the interest of medieval

scientists in infinity is a direct result of theological speculation. Pierre Sergescu has shown that it was the belief in an omnipotent God that required medieval thinkers to disagree with Aristotle's views on the infinite. Aristotle accepted the possibility of infinite divisibility but not of the infinitely large; Aquinas was constrained to argue that uncreated infinity exists and that it is within the power of God to create created infinity.[48]

The interaction between theology and mathematical speculation about infinity is the ground for greater precision in defining the referent for the endless geometrical figure. It is not only 'God' or 'Trinity' but God as absolute *veritas*. Nicholas of Cusa sums up his discussions of the connections between the Trinity and the infinite triangle (which must meet both the requirements of the *veritas trianguli* and the *veritas unitatis*) by saying

> Coniunge igitur ista, quae videntur opposita, antecedenter, ut praedixi; et non habebis unum et tria vel e converso, sed unitrinum seu triunum. Et ista est veritas absoluta.[49]

> If, as I have suggested, you begin by previously uniting the apparent contradictories, you will not have 1 and 3 or 3 and 1 but a 'unitrinity' or 'triunity.' That is infinite truth.[50]

Further, *veritas* is not simply the goal and product of the analysis of geometrical figures but is also the motive force for the inquiry as well as the referent for the first traditional analogy quoted by Nicholas:

> Ita igitur agentes et sub directione maximae veritatis incipientes dicimus, quod sancti viri et elevatissimi ingenii, qui se figuris applicarunt, variae locuti sunt: Anselmus devotissimus veritatem maximam rectitudini infinitae comparavit.[51]

> By this method, and guided by Infinite Truth, we note the difference of expressions used by saintly men and brilliant intellects who gave themselves to the study of figures. St. Anselm, for example, compared Absolute truth to infinite straightness.[52]

Though it is perhaps not just to treat Anselm's extensive discussion of the nature of *Summa Veritas* in such a cursory fashion, he does

indeed argue that *veritas* is quintessentially endless. In fact his belief
in the demonstrable endlessness of *Summa Veritas* is the ground
for his view that *Summa Natura* is endless:

> Si summa illa natura principium vel finem habet, non est vera aeterni-
> tas, quod esse supra inexpugnabiliter inventum esse. Deinde cogitet
> qui potest, quando incepit aut quando non fuit hoc verum: scilicet quia
> futurum erat aliquid; aut quando desinet et non erit hoc verum:
> videlicet quia praeteritum erit aliquid. Quodsi neutrum horum cogitari
> potest, et utrumque hoc verum sine veritate esse non potest: impossi-
> bile est vel cogitare, quod veritas principium aut finem habeat. Denique
> si veritas habuit principium vel habebit finem: antequam ipsa inciperet,
> verum erat tunc quia non erat veritas: et postquam finita erit, verum
> erit tunc quia non erit veritas. Atqui verum non potest esse sine
> veritate. Erat igitur veritas, antequam esset veritas; et erit veritas, po-
> stquam finita erit veritas: quod inconvenientissimum est. Sive igitur di-
> catur veritas habere, sive intelligatur non habere principium vel finem:
> nullo claudi potest veritas principio vel fine. Quare idem sequitur de
> summa natura, quia ipsa summa veritas est.[53]

Moreover if the Supreme Nature were to have a beginning or an end
it would not be true eternity – something which we have already
uncontestably found it to be. Or again, let anyone who can, try to
conceive of when it began to be true, or was ever not true, that
something was going to exist. Or [let him try to conceive of] when it
will cease being true and will not be true that something has existed
in the past. Now if neither of these things can be conceived, and if
both statements can be true only if there is truth, then it is impossible
even to think that truth has a beginning or an end. Indeed, suppose
that truth had had a beginning, or suppose that it would at some
time come to an end: Then even before truth had begun to be, it
would have been true that there was no truth; and even after truth
had come to an end, it would still be true that there would be no
truth. But it could not be true without truth. Hence, there would
have been truth before truth came to be, and there would still be
truth after truth had ceased to be. But these conclusions are self-
contradictory. Therefore, whether truth is said to have a beginning or
an end, or whether it is understood not to have a beginning or an
end, truth cannot be confined by any beginning or end. Consequently,

the same conclusion holds with regard to the Supreme Nature, because the Supreme Nature is the Supreme Truth.[54]

In this tradition of infinite geometry, the qualities of an endless figure as a *res* make it an appropriate *signum* for absolute *veritas*. The first institutor displayed his use of right reason by imposing a sign whose visible properties correspond to the invisible properties of its referent. Just as the figure is without beginning or end, so too *veritas* is without beginning or end. The figure is simultaneously unified and composite, and *veritas* is One and yet manifested in many, in creatures and propositions. An infinite figure is, *secundum ymaginacionem mathematicam*, a contradiction in terms, and the *veritas* it signifies unites maximum and minimum and has no beginning or end even if we start from the hypothesis that it has a beginning or an end.

2   The *Significatio* of *Trawþ*

The pentangle as described by the *Gawain* poet shares these essential features with the speculative geometers' endless figures. It too is without beginning or end, and it is simultaneously unified and composite, and it is a contradiction in terms. On these grounds alone we would be justified in equating them and therefore their referents, but there is additional supporting evidence from the poet's choice of the word *trawþ* as a label for the quality that the pentangle represents. The OED lists two new, interrelated senses for *trawþ* from the fourteenth century: '9. True religious belief or doctrine; orthodoxy,' and '10. That which is true, real, or actual (in a general or abstract sense); reality; *spec.* in religious use, spiritual reality as the subject of revelation or object of faith.' While the older words, *sooth* and its derivatives, continue in use (for example, in Chaucer's *Boece*), *trawþ* becomes the favoured equivalent for *veritas* in a theological sense. A brief examination of the concordance to the Vulgate shows that the medieval translators of the Bible generally used *trawþ* for *veritas*, as these most obvious examples of the absolute sense show:

> Dicit ei Iesus: Ego sum via, et veritas, et vita. Nemo venit ad Patrem, nisi per me. Ioh. 14:6[55]

ihesus seith to him/ I am weye truthe and liif/ no man cometh to
the fadir: but bi me.[56]

Ego in hoc natus sum, et ad hoc venio in mundum, ut testimonium
perhibeam veritati: omnis qui est ex veritate, audit vocem meam.
Dicit et Pilatus: Quid est veritas? Ioh. 18:37–8

I am comen in to the world to bere witnessynge to truthe/ eche that
is of truthe herith my vois/ pilat seith to hym/ what is truthe?

et cognoscetis veritatem, et veritas liberabit vos. Ioh. 8:32

and ȝe schuln knowe the truthe: and the truthe schal make ȝou fre.

When Reginald Pecock is describing what God is 'as he is, verrili
in himsilf,' his list of infinities ends: 'infinite good, infinite maiestful,
infinite fair, myri *and* swete, infinite myȝti, wijs *and* louyng, infinite mercyful, piteful *and* desirose, infinite large, fre *and* gentil, infinite trew *and* infinite trowþe.'[57] The author of *Dives and Pauper*
frequently refers to the fact that God is 'souereyn trewþe' and speaks
of 'God wose name is trewþe.'[58] The Carmelite Richard Lavynham
speaks against covetous traitors who 'for loue of þe money sell
þe trewthe & god him self is trewth.'[59] A sermon from ms Royal 18
B xxiii, in describing the fall of Adam, reminds us that 'God is
trowthe, and all trowthe commeþ of hym.'[60]
    With the correspondences between the pentangle as a *signum* and
the infinite figures of the geometers established and with the equation between their referents uncovered, we may summarize the work
of the *Gawain* poet in the realm of pure signification. The pentangle, as a sign set by Solomon at a particular point in time, is a
signum ad placitum according to the definitions used by the terminist logicians whose writings were in use in the poet's era. *Ad placitum* does not mean that it is an arbitrary sign (although Burrow
seems to view the phrase in that way[61]), for this sign has been imposed in accordance with Lambert of Auxerre's *recta ratio*, since
it is a stable sign imposed because of a similarity between it and its
referent. Its spatial endlessness, its combination of the composite
and the unified, and its reconciliation of apparent contradictories are
all analogous to the properties of *Summa Veritas*. Both the pentangle and the word *trawþ* therefore signify Absolute Truth.

2 The Uses of a Sign

The argument of the preceding chapter has led to a conclusion that, on the face of it, is contrary to the views of all previous readings. We all know that the pentangle, whatever its origin and whatever its characteristics, means something about Gawain. This would, I expect, lead my readers to respond, "It is not this at all." But medieval sign theory was much less rigid and exclusive in some senses than modern notions about meaning. If, for example, a word is attached to one referent in one sentence and another referent in another sentence, we would say that it has one meaning in the first case and another meaning in the second. The medieval distinction between *significatio* and *suppositio* allows for greater flexibility. There are, of course, cases where the word is said to have two or more different and unrelated significations: the usual example of this is *canis*, the word for dog. It can refer either to the animal that barks, a particular kind of fish, or the star Sirius. In other cases of this phenomenon (called *equivocatio*), there is a definite connection between the various significations. The word *healthy* has different meanings in the sentences 'The urine is healthy,' 'This food is healthy,' and 'This man is healthy,' but the meanings are related: 'indicative of health,' 'productive of health' and 'possessing health.'[1]

Words do not therefore lose their *significatio* when they are used in propositions, although the nature of the proposition could well indicate which of several significations may be operative. Nor should the pentangle be considered to have lost its primary signification when it is bodied forth in a "proposition" about Gawain, although its full force will obviously be somewhat different from the force of the pentangle in isolation. This transition, from abstract sign to element in a proposition about an individual human being, results from the poet's particular ability to construct a narrative out of static materials. He is not writing a purely encyclopaedic work like the *De Proprietatibus* of Barthlomaeus Anglicus, nor is he presenting a linear work of philosophic argumentation, like Nicholas of Cusa. For them the pentangle would have been an object of contemplation and a focus for a purely intellectual experience. The *Gawain* poet brings the concept it signifies into a human and historical world, and so provokes an examination not only of the absolute truth it signifies but also of the complex relationship between that absolute and the relative, temporal world of human values.

In order to effect this enlargement of the possibilities of communication by means of this sign in its various contexts, the poet utilizes not only the secondary elaborations of the logicians' sign theory but also his audience's knowledge of and interest in a more chivalric signification system, that of contemporary heraldry. As a pure sign the pentangle relates to a transcendent and timeless truth; as a mark on Gawain's shield it is more like a label for a particular man. The background for an understanding of its full meaning therefore lies in the coincidence of medieval ideas about signs in general, heraldic devices, and proper names. Here too, however, the poet was not working in a vacuum: there are many comparable examples from his age that can be used to learn the standard assumptions about the uses of signs referring to particular individuals and reveal something about their natures.

B   THE HERALDIC SIGN AS TOKEN OF THE BEARER

It is clear that a man's heraldic device was seen in the medieval period as a simple sign for the man himself. As such it was given a great deal of importance and treated with much more attention than any practical purpose would warrant. As Rodney Dennys explains,

> The ensigns or cognisances painted upon their shields had a much greater significance to the men of the Middle Ages than we, in this less imaginative age, usually appreciate. Ramón Lull laid great stress on the significance and symbolism of knighthood. The ceremony of creating a new knight had, by his time [ca. 1235–1315], taken on something of the nature of a sacrament in which the Church

took an active part; and the ceremonial presentation to the new knight of his sword, spurs and shield, such as took place when King Henry I knighted Count Geoffrey of Anjou, gave rise to a particular symbolism in which feudal obligation, the calls of religion, and social duty were interwoven. It can therefore be seen that the device on a knight's shield would have a special significance and be regarded by him and his followers as his 'alter ego.'[2]

Heraldic devices were not limited to body armour and other military equipment but were often placed on personal property as a sign of ownership. Such marks were not assigned only to fighting men, for we find heraldic coats of arms ascribed to both clerics and women.

In many late medieval works a man's armour is explicitly pointed out as a means of recognition when his identity is not otherwise determinable. In *Dives and Pauper*, for example, there is a story about a man who disobeyed his uncle's deathbed request that he sell a favourite horse and give the money to the poor. While riding the horse later on, he was carried away by fiends and not found until four days later, his body rent limb from limb. Though the corpse was unrecognizable, 'by hys cote armure þei knewyn wel þat it was þe same man.'[3]

The same situation prevails in the epic literature popular in the period, where problems of recognizing friends during the chaos of battle are raised only to be solved by a herald's expertise. In *The Sege off Melayne*, for example, there is a passage describing how Bishop Turpin, in the heat of battle, mistakes Breton reinforcements for Saracens and attacks. Despite his "blody wedes" he is recognized, not by his personal appearance but by the device on his shield:

So blody was that Bischoppis wede
His conysaunce ne ȝit his stede
Þe Bretons ne couthe noghte knawe.
Bot als an harawde hym by-helde
He lukede vp in to his schelde,
And sayde to all one rawe:
'If Bischoppe Turpyn appon lyve be,
In faythe, lordynges, ȝone es he
Þat ȝe se hedirwarde drawe.'

The bishop's clothes were so covered with blood that the Bretons were unable to recognize his device or his horse. But when a herald saw him, he looked at his shield and said to all of them, 'If Bishop Turpin is alive, in faith, my lords, that is he, whom you see coming this way.'

The skill of the professional herald at reading and deciphering the signs has saved the day, and all that remains is for the Bretons to identify themselves in order to prevent the attack by the furious Turpin. This too is accomplished by recourse to a conventional sign rather than through any transfer of personal information, as one of the soldiers calls out the French army's battle cry:

> 'A Mounte Ioye,' cryes one þat he myghte here,
> He was glad of þat sawe.[4]

One of them cried out 'Mounjoy' so that he could hear, and he was glad of that saying.

People are known in the world of epic battle by sign and countersign, and the presuppositions of the signifying system are left unquestioned.
    A quite different situation may be found in the medieval romance tradition, where one of the underlying assumptions has always been that there is more to a man than can be seen and certainly more than can be accounted for by social institutions. Not surprisingly, many romances contain scenes that address the problems within heraldic signification systems more directly and demonstrate that simple knowledge of outward signs is not sufficient for an understanding of the inner reality. An example of such a scene occurs in *Sir Perceval of Galles*, where Gawain confronts a warrior wearing armour that he believes to be Perceval's, and yet is unwilling to assume that the knight is actually Perceval:

> Þogfe Perceval hase slayne þe rede knyght,
> 3itt may anoþer be als wyghte
> And in þat gere be dyghte,
> And taken alle him fra.
> If I suffire my sister-sone,
> And anothir in his gere be done
> And gete þe maystry me appon,
> Þat wolde do me wa.

Though Perceval has slain the Red Knight, still another man could

be dressed in that armour, having taken it from him. If I yield to
him, as if to my sister's son, and another is wearing his clothing, and
so gets the mastery of me, that would make me sad.

And so they fight. The disaster of kin-slaughter is avoided when
they finally recognize each other, not through heraldic signs but by
voice and personal information. The recognition is ultimately capped
by a reference to shared personal experience, as Gawain says:

> I ame no sowdane,
> Bot I am þat ilke man,
> Þat thi bodi by-gan,
> In armours to dighte.[5]

I am no sultan, but I am the very man who first caused you to be
clothed in armour.

The contradiction implicit in heraldic practice, that the device is not
the man but may be taken for the man, is confronted directly in
this scene so that a different notion of what constitutes a man may
be put forward: the signifying relationship between man and mark
is stretched to the breaking-point.

The *Gawain* poet seems to me to be operating within this romance
tradition but to have a subtler approach to the problems it faces.
Instead of simply abandoning the epic assumptions about the equation between the man and his heraldic sign, he is able, as we shall
see, to experiment with the traditional assumptions and their parallels in logical sign theory in order to express an even fuller notion
of the identity of his hero.

C   THE HERALDIC SIGN AS *SIGNUM*

1   The Origins of Heraldry

There is general agreement among medieval and modern treatises
about the original purpose of heraldic insignia. Though the modern
authors are coolly rationalistic and the medieval writers tend to ro-
manticize, both agree that the purpose was, at the beginning, simply
to distinguish one warrior from another in the heat of battle. Julian
Franklyn offers the following explanation: 'When every face of
the field of battle was concealed by a steel mask, it became impossi-

ble to distinguish between friend and foe, and the rank and file could not be sure which of the totally enclosed warriors was their leader. This state of affairs was dangerous to both sides in the fray, and the need for an easily recognizable and distinct mark was established.'⁶

While such a pragmatic view may be sufficient to account for the fact that the different sides in a battle are conspicuously marked or that a commander should be recognizable as such, it does not explain the elaborate devices identifying individuals. A standard medieval treatise gives a more detailed historical justification, linking heraldry fancifully with the Trojan War and demonstrating the belief that desire for personal fame played an important role in the first assigning of devices:

> First, as herodes recorden, the beginninge and grownde of Armes was at the Sege of Troy, withinne the towne and withoute, because of the dughtynesse of the dedes that were shewed and done on both the parties, and because that ther was so grete a multitude opon both parties that one myght not be knowen from another of their poyntes of worshippe, caused the kynges withinne the towne and withoute to assemble togedir, and by their discrete aduyse concentid togedir and accordid, that euery mann that shuld to a poynt of worshippe shuld haue to hymself a marke of worshippe in tokyn of his dughtynes, that the poeple myght haue knowelage of hym.

It is further established that each man's sign must be similar to that of his immediate family, although differences must be added for further personal discrimination: 'The eldest son shuld haue a labell, the second son a cressent, the third son a molet, the fourt son a merlet, the v sonn an anulet, the vi sonn a floure de lyce. And if ther were any moo bredren then vi, then the fadir shuld giffe them what difference that shuld plese hym best.'⁷ What began as a simple expedient to distinguish warring factions from each other had become a signifying system that not only labelled individuals but conveyed information about their status.

2   The Mutability of the Heraldic Sign

Heraldic signs are said to be imposed, and so are not natural signs but rather *signa ad placitum*. Some examples of heraldic practice show further that the relationship between a man and his device is considerably less stable than the relationship between a word and its referent. While a man who inherited his coat of arms from his father and wore it without substantial change might well share the assumptions of the author of *The Sege off Melayne*, problems arose in the practice of heraldry that obliged the theorists to deal with the fact that the device was not a permanent sign.

Whenever a new knight was created, or whenever a knight decided that some change in his circumstances justified a new coat of arms, it would be obvious that the relationship between a man and his arms was conventional. King Richard I, for example, changed his arms from a single lion rampant to three lions rampant, and other men changed even more frequently: 'John Wrythe, the third Garter King of Arms (d. 1504) bore firstly Azure a Fess between three Doves close argent within a Bordure or; then he tried Azure three Doves close argent within a Royal Tressure or; but as Garter he used Azure a Cross or between four Doves close argent, beaks and legs gules.'[8] Since armour was differenced according to the bearer's place in the family, subtle modifications of arms would be common as various near relatives died. It has been suggested that the reference in *Sir Gawain* to the 'pentangel nwe' (636) means not only that the device was newly painted but also that it was newly imposed as a sign and that the author had just granted new arms to his hero.[9]

Just as one man might be symbolized by more than one device, so several men might, in theory, be symbolized by the same sign. This is no problem at all when considered as an analogy for the situation with verbal signs, for the terminists' understanding of *equivocatio* dealt with a parallel case regarding personal names:

> Tale autem aequivocum est duplex. Unum est aequivocum a casu, quando scilicet vox pluribus conceptibus subordinatur et ita uni, ac si non suboridinaretur alteri, et ita significat unum, ac si non significaret aliud; sicut est de hoc nomine 'Sortes,' quod imponitur pluribus hominibus.[10]

> There are, however, two types of equivocality. In the first case a term is equivocal by chance. Here a term is subordinated to several concepts, but it would be subordinated to one of these concepts even if it were not subordinated to the other(s); and similarly, it could signify one thing even if it did not signify the other(s). An example is the name Socrates, which is assigned to several men.[11]

While the heraldic manuals do assert that there are certain arms that are the exclusive, hereditary property of certain families, having

been granted by an emperor or a king, and also that there are circumstances under which the use of another man's arms constitutes
fraud, in general they work from the same principles as the logicians. Two men are allowed to bear the same arms, especially if they
choose them themselves:

> But if the King of France had given a silver lion to my line, what
> harm would result if Germans in Germany bore similar arms? They
> would certainly not be punished by law. We have also another
> kind of arms that a man assumes at his pleasure. You must know that
> men's names were invented to show the distinction between persons.
> Such names any man may choose at pleasure, either the father for
> his son or the godfather for his godson. And further, a man may
> change his name, provided he does not do so for purposes of fraud but
> merely to have a pleasanter name. The same is true of arms. So,
> such arms as may be chosen at pleasure each may take as he wishes,
> and may have them painted on his horse and on his belongings,
> but not on the belongings of others.[12]

Bartolo di Sassoferrato (1313–59), in his *De Insigniis et Armis*,
discusses the question with copious references to precedents in Ro-
man law concerning the use of other people's names and other
people's property, and decides that arms are more similar to names
than to property. He therefore concludes that they may be used
at will, provided that no injury is done thereby to another party:

> Ergo potest quis assumere arma aliena ... signum quod portat aliquis
> non est unum et idem, immo sunt diversa, habentia tamen omnimo-
> dam similitudinem. Ad decisionem ergo praedictorum praemitto,
> quod signum alienum portare potest prohibere seu petere ut prohi-
> beatur ille cuius est signum, si ex hoc ipse iniurietur, quia forte
> ille cum vituperio portat vel vituperiose tractat arma.[13]

> Therefore one man can assume another's arms ... The signs people
> wear are not numerically identical, but diverse, though they resemble
> each other in every particular. Therefore I argue the view of the
> aforementioned experts, that a sign's owner may prohibit or ask that
> it be prohibited that someone wear his sign only if he is injured
> by the wearing, since the other man may wear it in a blameworthy
> way or handle the arms shamefully.

Subject to these restrictions, which do not bear on the question of *significatio*, the heraldic sign is considered to be attached to its referent in a purely conventional way. In practice a man may have more than one sign, just as a thing may be signified by more than one word; similarly, a sign may be attached to more than one man, just as a word may refer to a variety of things. The heraldic device therefore bears all the marks of a *signum ad placitum*.

3   Imposition According to Qualities

Nevertheless, many heraldic signs do seem to be more stable than we might expect if they were purely a matter of whim. After all, as the *Tretis on Armes* explains, they were first instituted by men who used 'discrete aduyse,' which is surely an English equivalent of Lambert's *recta ratio*. Even though Richard I made changes in his coat of arms, he always kept the lion, and John Wrythe kept the dove. In at least these two cases, then, it was felt that there was a similarity between the qualities of the man and of his mark, for the lion refers to Richard's nickname 'the Lion-hearted' and to his courage, and the dove was considered appropriate to a herald because of its abilities as a messenger.

Just as in the case of words that are imposed according to qualities, the most obvious examples of this phenomenon in heraldry are those grounded in a sort of etymology. The earliest suggested example is the helmet of King Arthur mentioned in both Geoffrey of Monmouth's *Historia Regum Britanniae* and Wace's *Brut*. It is decorated with a dragon, which may be a reference to Arthur's father, Uther Pendragon.[14] Such canting arms, which involve a punning reference to the bearer's family name, proliferate during the following centuries. Chess rooks are used by families named De Rochis, De Rechis, and Di Rechis, and are ascribed to the King of Morocco.[15] Geoffrey Plantagenet earned his nickname from the fact that he carried a sprig of broom (*genet*) on his helmet;[16] his descendants used not only broom but also a weasel (also *genet*) as heraldic devices. Some references become quite recondite:

> The Harrington knot is simply a fret but it probably has a canting
> significance: the fret is a combination of mascules, the mascule
> is a mesh, mesh constitutes nets, nets take fish, and the fish of first
> importance is the herring, hence *herring–Harrington*.[17]

Some puns of this kind seem obscure to us merely because the punning words are obsolete or dialectical or foreign, such as the monastery or *moustier* of Musters, the *bourdons* or staves of Burdon, the *bosons* or bird bolts of Boson, the *gurges* or whirlpool of Gorges, and the *herisons* or hedgehogs of Herries.[18]

In addition to such puns on the owner's family name or nickname, a connection between a man and his arms is often a reference to his occupation. Franklyn refers, for example, to the use of Noah's ark in the arms of the Company of Shipwrights,[19] but loftier social functions are often alluded to as well: 'Argentine probably bore covered cups in allusion to his tenure by the service of providing a silver cup for the coronation, while Butler bore them in allusion to the office indicated by his name, even as Chamberlain bore keys.'[20] Animals worn as armorial devices were thought to reflect on the personalities of their owners. A dog signifies a faithful warrior, says Johannes de Bado Aureo (circa 1394); a horse is a sign of a man eager for battle, and a swan signifies a singer. Such associations are often validated by reference to appropriate authorities:

> Columba ... est pacis nuntia et laetitiae, ut patet in Gen., capitulo viii° ... Est etiam naturaliter timida, raro secura nisi in foramine, et est valde obliviosa. Haec Ieronimus, et concordat Aristoteles, Libro vi°. Columbam portare igitur est signum simplicitatis, et quod portans plus confidit in sociis suis quam in propria fortitudine. Et columbam in armis portare bene pertinere solet ad haraldos armorum, qui dimissa arte sua sibi et suis arma assumunt; et dicit Ieronimus in libro iv° quod in Aegypto et in Syria instruitur columba ut litterarum sit baiula de una provincia in aliam. Et cum illo concordat Bartholomaeus, *De Proprietatibus Rerum*, libro xii°, capitulo vii°.[21]

> The dove is a messenger of peace and joy, as is clear in chapter 8 of Genesis. It is also naturally timid, rarely secure except in its home, and very forgetful, according to Jerome, and Aristotle agrees in book 6. To wear a dove is therefore a sign of simplicity, and a sign that the bearer trusts more in his companions than in his own strength. And it is generally quite appropriate for heralds to bear doves on their arms if they give up their art and assume arms for themselves and their families; and Jerome says in book 4 that in Egypt and Syria a dove is taught to be a carrier of letters from one province to another. And Bartholomaeus agrees with him in book 12, chapter 7, of *De Proprietatibus Rerum*.

Like other *signa ad placitum*, therefore, the heraldic device accords with the qualities of its referent and so may be profitably used as a starting-point for determining those qualities.

D   THE ENDLESS FIGURE AS A SIGN FOR A HUMAN

I   Sacred Heraldry

The pentangle is far from being the only sign for the divine that is used as a heraldic symbol in the medieval period. Rather, we find examples of arms attributed to Christ, to Mary and the saints, to God the Father, to angels, and to the Trinity, all from a fairly early date. One such symbol is described as follows from a modern handbook of heraldry: 'Azure, four plates, one in dexter-chief, one in sinister-chief, one on the fess point, one in centre-base all conjoined by both an orle and a pall argent. On fess-point the word, "Deus"; dexter-chief, "Pater"; sinister-chief, "Filius"; centre-base, "Sanctus spiritus." On the three limbs of the pall, "est"; on the three elements of the orle, "non est"; in expression of the Trinity.'[22]
This device (see Figure 4) is both composite and unified in that it is formed out of six separate and even mutually contradictory propositions, namely:

> The Father is not the Holy Spirit
> The Son is not the Father
> The Holy Spirit is not the Son
> The Father is God
> The Son is God
> The Holy Spirit is God

but yet it is unified for those who recognize it as an expression of theological truth. Each proposition 'vmbelappez and loukez in oþer,'' and though each term is written only once, it participates in three propositions. Its endlessness and its apparent internal contradictions make it an appropriate visible sign for the Trinity, a verbal description of which is considerably more complex and cumbersome:

> Ita pater et filius et spiritus sanctus et singulus quisque horum deus
> et simul omnes unus deus, et singulus quisque horum plena substantia et simul omnes una substantia. Pater nec filius est nec spiritus
> sanctus, filius nec pater est nec spiritus sanctus, spiritus sanctus nec
> pater nec filius, sed pater tantum pater et filius tantum filius et

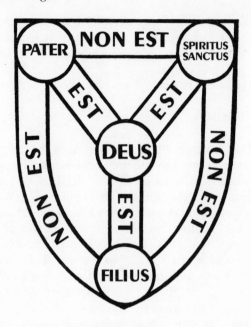

Figure 4 The Shield of Truth

spiritus sanctus tantum spiritus sanctus. Eadem tribus aeternitas, eadem incommutabilitas, eadem maiestas, eadem potestas. In patre unitas, in filio aequalitas, in spiritu sancto unitatis aequalitatisque concordia, et tria haec unum omnia propter patrem, aequalia omnia propter filium, conexa omnia propter spiritum sanctum.[23]

Thus there are the Father, the Son, and the Holy Spirit, and each is God, and at the same time all are one God; and each of them is a full substance, and at the same time all are one substance. The Father is neither the Son nor the Holy Spirit; the Son is neither the Father nor the Holy Spirit; the Holy Spirit is neither the Father nor the Son. But the Father is the Father uniquely; the Son is the Son uniquely; and the Holy Spirit is the Holy Spirit uniquely. All three have the same eternity, the same immutability, the same majesty, and the same power. In the Father is unity, in the Son equality, and in the Holy Spirit a concord of unity and equality; and these three qualities are all one because of the Father, all equal because of the Son, and all united because of the Holy Spirit.[24]

This same set of arms is ascribed to Christ in *Piers Plowman*:

'What berþ þat buyrn,' quod I þo, 'so blisse þee bitide?'
'Thre leodes in oon lyth, noon lenger þan ooþer,
Of oon muchel and myght in mesure and lengþe.
That oon dooþ alle dooþ and each dooþ bi his one.
The firste haþ myȝt and maiestee, makere of alle þynges;
Pater is his propre name, a persone by hymselue.
The second of þa[t] sire is Sothfastnesse *filius*,
Wardeyn of þat wit haþ; was euere wiþouten gynnyng.
The þridde highte þe holi goost, a persone by hymselue,
The light of al þat lif haþ a londe and a watre,
Confortour of creatures; of hym comeþ alle blisse.'[25]

'What arms does that man wear, as bliss awaits you?'
    'Three persons in one body, none longer than the other, of one size
and power in measure and length. They all do what one of them
does, and each acts by himself. The first has power and majesty, the
creator of all things, a person by himself, and Father is his proper
name. The second is the Son of that Father, called Truth, the guardian
of what has wit, and he existed always, without beginning. The
third is called the Holy Ghost, a person by himself, the light of all
that has life on land and water, the comforter of all creatures,
and from him comes all bliss.'

    Another set of arms frequently attributed to Christ is based not on
the mystery of the Trinity but on the crucifixion. Such a shield
depicts the Cross, three nails, the lance, the crown of thorns,
scourges, and the sponge: 'We soon find the Instruments of the
Passion being depicted on armorial shields and it is evident that they
were regarded as the especial emblems of Our Lord and personal to
him in the same way as a coat of arms. There is early evidence
that these 'Arma Christi,' sometimes called the 'Scutum Salvationis'
or Arms of Salvation, were held to be heraldic, for there is a Book of
Hours of the early fourteenth century in the Bibliothèque de
l'Arsenal, which describes them in heraldic terms.'[26] A fourteenth-
century English sermon describes a different coat of arms with a
similar meaning. The preacher tells an allegorical story about a hermit who meets a knight whose coat of arms is 'a beere of blake
with a lylie of white and v roses of redde.' The hermit, we are told,
is every Christian, and the knight is Christ himself:

> But what bare he in is armys? A beere of blake, þe wiche was bittur
> penaunce þat he suffred on þe Rode Tre; a lilie of whyte, þat was
> is own preciouse bodye in all is bittur penaunce; v roses of rede, þe
> wiche were þe v princypall woundes in ys bodye.[27]

> But what did he bear on his armour? A bier of black, which was the
> bitter penance that he suffered on the cross; a white lily, which
> was his own precious body in all his bitter penance; five red roses,
> which were the five principal wounds in his body.

As these examples show, then, there was no real innovation on
the part of the *Gawain* poet when he decided to use the pentangle
sign of absolute truth as a heraldic device. As a mark on a shield
it is a visible reminder of the truth of the Trinity, unified, composite,
and endless like the Trinity itself. The difficulty and hence the
poetic utility of his poetic decision comes from the fact that it is
ascribed in the poem not to the Trinity or to Christ but to Gawain.

2   The Problem of Deification

Is it permissible to assign to a man a sign that signifies God? It
would seem at first glance that, in the use of the pentangle as a
man's ensign, there is something dangerous about the apparent
equation of the human and the divine, for there is surely no more
persistent idea in the medieval period than that man is not God and
that the distinction between the Creator and his creatures is absolute. Nevertheless, there are strong indications that this gulf was not
considered to be totally unbridgeable. Quite apart from the fact
that there is a mediator in the person of the Word made flesh, we
must deal with a number of biblical texts that suggest that ordinary
men may become gods, or sons of God, or like God, and that indeed
require that they should make the effort. These texts and the way
in which they come to be understood in the medieval period are of
great assistance in discovering the nature of the relationship
between Gawain's personal qualities and the qualities of the divine
Truth that is the appropriate first referent for the pentangle.

A history of the exegesis of Psalm 81, a statement about the lot of
unjust judges, would provide a great deal of information about
attitudes towards the relationship between the divine and the human.
The psalm as a whole reads as follows:

1 Deus stetit in synagoga deorum,
  In medio autem deos diiudicat.
2 Usquequo iudicatis iniquitatem,
  Et facies peccatorum sumitis?
3 Iudicate egeno et pupillo;
  Humilem et pauperem iustificate.
4 Eripite pauperem,
  Et egenum de manu peccatoris liberate.
5 Nescierunt, neque intellexerunt,
  In tenebris ambulant;
  Movebuntur omnia fundamenta terrae.
6 Ego dixi: Dii estis,
  Et filii Excelsi omnes.
7 Vos autem sicut homines moriemini,
  Et sicut unus de principibus cadetis.
8 Surge, Deus, iudica terram,
  Quoniam tu haereditatabis in omnibus gentibus.

1 God hath stood in the congregation of gods: and being in the midst of them he judgeth gods.
2 How long will you judge unjustly: and accept the persons of the wicked?
3 Judge for the needy and the fatherless: do justice to the humble and the poor.
4 Rescue the poor; and deliver the needy out of the hand of the sinner.
5 They have not known nor understood: they walk on in darkness: all the foundations of the earth shall be moved.
6 I have said: You are gods and all of you the sons of the most High.
7 But you like men shall die: and shall fall like one of the princes.
8 Arise, O God, judge thou the earth: for thou shalt inherit among all the nations.

The main difficulty with this psalm, for all later commentators, is the identity of the other 'gods.' Modern biblical scholars reject the idea that they are humans, either the judges of Israel or rulers of nations who are oppressing Israel, and suggest that they are rather 'the national gods of various peoples of the world, who have been demoted to the position of Yahweh's servants.' Though God 'once thought that you were divine beings and that you would act as such,'[28] their improper behaviour as judges leads God to threaten them with the loss of their divine status and even of their existence. Verse 6, it is claimed, has a slightly ironical tone.

Such an interpretation was, of course, unavailable to a medieval thinker. The existence of foreign gods was denied, as, I think, was the possibility that God might be joking in recording a decree in as solemn a form as 'Ego dixi.' Christ, in John 10:32–5, explicitly declared that the "dii" were a group of humans, but this historical reference to a particular group of Israelite judges was of little use to the later exegetical tradition, and the psalm came to be interpreted not simply as a condemnation of one group but as a discriminating judgment between two groups. Aided by a slight mistranslation in the *Vulgate* ('Vos autem' has been replaced by 'Verumtamen' in the new Latin version approved by Pius XII in 1954), medieval interpreters, following Augustine, saw verse 6 as a reference to the elect and verse 7 as a condemnation of the damned:

> Sive ad illos dixerit, *Ego dixi, Dii estis, et filii Altissimi omnes*, ad eos qui praedestinati sunt in vitam aeternam ... *vos autem* per infirmitatem carnis, *sicut homines moriemini, et,* per elationem animi, *sicut unus ex principibus,* id est diabolus, non extollemini, sed *cadetis.*[29]

> Whether to those he said this, 'I said, Ye are gods,' to those particularly who are predestined to eternal life ... 'but ye,' through the infirmity of your flesh, 'shall die like men,' and through haughtiness of soul, 'like one of the princes,' that is, the devil, shall not be exalted, but 'shall fall.'[30]

This division, between those who are predestined for salvation and those who fall after trying to exalt themselves, is graphically depicted in the initial illustration for this psalm in the *St Alban's Psalter*, which shows Christ in a temple with a sword. There are two figures in front of him, whom he is addressing, and two behind him, at whom he points his sword: 'The psalm is a prayer to God to judge between the just and the unjust. Clearly the two figures, on whom His face is turned, represent the blessed, and the two on whom His back is turned are the damned for whom the sword is prepared. This is the sword which St Augustine explains in a different context as the one brought by Christ to separate the faithful from the unfaithful.'[31]

This psalm is given the same reading by the author of the four-teenth-century *Pricke of Conscience*, who quotes verses 6 and 7 in widely separate sections of his poem. He describes first the error and punishment of those who pay too little attention to God:

Many synful has her na grace
To haf tyme of repentance, ne space;
For whiles þai lyf þai have na mynde
Of God, bot forgettes hym, als ay unkynde.
Me thyn[k] þan þat it es skille and right
Þat thurgh dede God reve þam mynd and myght;
Þus sal þai dyghe and heven blis tyne
And be putted til endeles pyne,
Þat til God here er swa uncurtays,
Þarfor David in þe psauter says:
Vos sicut homines moriemini, et
sicut unus de principibus cadetis.
He says: 'Als men yhe sal digh alle,
And als ane of þe princes yhe sal falle.'
Þat es yhe sal dighe of þe same manere,
Als men dighes in þis world here,
And als þe spyrites þat fra heven felle,
Be casten don intille helle.[32]

Many sinners do not have grace here to have time or space for repentance. While they live they take no thought for God, but forget him, quite unnaturally. I think that it is proper and right that through death God should deprive them of mind and might; thus those who are uncourteous to God here shall die and lose heaven's bliss and be put into endless pain. Therefore David, in the Psalter, says, 'As men you shall all die, and as one of the princes you shall fall.' That is, you will die in the same manner as men die in this world here, and, like the spirits that fell from heaven, you shall be cast down into hell.

The rewards of the psalm's previous verse are later promised to the righteous:

Þus wyse salle þai be þat salle come
Tylle þe kyngdom of heven, after þe dome.
Þai salle be Godes sons, and tille him lyke,

And be made his heyres of hevenryke,
And be alle als Godes of gret myght,
Als þe prophet, in þe psauter, says ryght:
Ego dixi: 'Dii estis et
filii excelsi omnes.'
He says: 'I sayd, "yhe er Godes alle
And Godes sons men salle yhow calle." '
Wharfor it semes, þat when þai com
Tylle heven, þai salle be fulle of wysdom
And fulle of myght, lastand ever-mare,
When þai salle alle be als Godes þare.[33]

Thus will those be who shall come to the kingdom of heaven after
the judgment. They shall be God's sons, and like him, and be made
heirs to the kingdom of heaven, and be like gods of great power,
as the prophet correctly says in the Psalter: 'I said, "You are all gods
and men will call you God's sons." ' Therefore it seems that when
they come to heaven they will be full of wisdom and full of might,
lasting ever more, when they will all be like gods there.

A number of similar biblical texts hold forth the promise that
certain men may be considered as sons of God. In Luke's Gospel it
would seem to be a reward for good works (Luke 6:34–6), but in the
Johannine books the emphasis is, characteristically enough, on
faith and the acceptance of Christ:

Quotquot autem receperunt eum,
Dedit eis potestatem filios Dei fieri,
His qui credunt in nomine eius:
Qui non ex sanguinibus,
Neque ex voluntate carnis,
Neque ex voluntate viri,
Sed ex Deo nati sunt.   (Ioh 1:12–13)

But as many as received him, he gave them power to be made the
sons of God, to them that believe in his name. Who are born, not of
blood, nor of the will of the flesh, nor of the will of man, but of God.

Videte qualem charitatem dedit nobis Pater, ut filii Dei nominemur
et simus. Propter hoc mundus non novit nos: quia non novit eum.
Charissimi, nunc filii Dei sumus: et nondum apparuit quod erimus.

Scimus quoniam cum apparuerit, similes ei erimus: quoniam videbi-
mus eum sicuti est. Et omnis qui habet hanc spem in eo, sanctificat
se, sicut et ille sanctus est.   (1 Ioh 3:1–3)

Behold what manner of charity the Father hath bestowed upon us,
that we should be called, and should be the sons of God. Therefore
the world knoweth not us, because it knew not him. Dearly beloved,
we are now the sons of God; and it hath not yet appeared what we
shall be. We know, that, when he shall appear, we shall be like
to him: because we shall see him as he is. And every one that hath
this hope in him, sanctifieth himself, as he also is holy.

Another such text makes reference to a quality, possessible by
both man and God, that has been more frequently used in *Gawain*
criticism, and that is 'perfection.' Matthew quotes Christ calling
on men to be 'perfecti' and not merely 'misericordes':

Ego autem dico vobis: Diligite inimicos vestros, benefacite his qui
oderunt vos: et orate pro persequentibus et calumniantibus vos:
ut sitis filii Patris vestri, qui in caelis est: qui solem suum oriri facit
super bonos et malos: et pluit super iustos et iniustos. Si enim
diligitis eos qui vos diligunt, quam mercedem habebitis? nonne et
publicani hoc faciunt? Et si salutaveritis fratres vestros tantum, quid
amplius facitis? nonne et ethnici hoc faciunt? Estote ergo vos perfecti, sicut et Pater vester caelestis perfectus est.   (Matt. 5:44–8)

But I say to you, Love your enemies: do good to them that hate you:
and pray for them that persecute and calumniate you: That you
may be the children of your Father who is in heaven, who maketh
his sun to rise upon the good, and bad, and raineth upon the just and
the unjust. For if you love them that love you, what reward shall
you have? do not even the publicans this? And if you salute your
brethren only, what do you more? do not also the heathens this?
Be you therefore perfect, as also your heavenly Father is perfect.

3   The Circumstances of Deification

Under certain circumstances, then, it is possible for a man to be the
son of God, to be like God, to be perfect as God is perfect, and,
indeed, to be called 'god,' that is, to be signified by a sign for God.
The interesting point for this study arises in connection with the

phrase 'under certain circumstances,' for medieval logicians were
quite sensitive to the distinction between a proposition that is true
simpliciter and one that is true only *secundum quid*. The *locus
classicus* for this distinction is in Aristotle's *On Sophistical
Refutations*:

> Fallacies connected with the use of some particular expression
> absolutely [that is, *simpliciter*] or in a certain respect [that is, *secun-
> dum quid*] and not in its proper sense, occur when that which is
> predicated in part only is taken as though it was predicated abso-
> lutely. For example, 'If that-which-is-not is an object of opinion, then
> that-which-is-not is'; for it is not the same thing 'to be something'
> and 'to be' absolutely ... In like manner when something is predicated
> in a certain respect and absolutely; for example, 'If an Indian, being
> black all over, is white in respect of his teeth, then he is white
> and not white.'[34]

Examples of similar troublesome syllogisms are found throughout
the teaching books and manuals of the late medieval logicians.
Lambert considers, for example, 'Ethiops est albus secundum dentes,
ergo est albus' (an Ethiopian is white with respect to his teeth,
therefore he is white), 'Chimera est ens opinabile, ergo est ens' (The
chimera is an imaginable being, therefore it is a being), and 'bonum
est ieiunare in quadragesima, ergo bonum est ieiunare' (it is good to
fast in Lent, therefore it is good to fast).[35] The *Summa Sophisticorum Elenchorum* examines 'monachi dormiunt in nocte, ergo dormiunt' (the monks sleep at night; therefore they [are] sleep[ing]), and
then offers a detailed explanation of the theoretical problems of
this type of fallacy with a syllogism about a great poet:

> quicumque est poeta magnus, ipse est magnus
> sed Spina est poeta magnus
> ergo Spina est magnus.
> Sophisma est secundum quid et simpliciter, quia non si '*magnus*'
> cum hac determinatione '*poeta*' predicatur de Spina et simpliciter
> predicatur '*magnus.*' Ibi enim est accidentalis predicatio, quia '*mag-
> nus*' secundum accidens predicatur de Spina. Et ideo non sequitur.
> Videtur tamen quod hoc nomen '*magnus*' mutet significationem ex
> diversis adiunctis, quia cum dicitur: '*Spina est poeta magnus,*' id
> est *est magnus in poetria*; sed cum dicitur simpliciter '*Spina est*

magnus,' id est: *magnus in corpore.* Et secundum hoc videtur quod
hic paralogismus sit in tertio modo equivocationis.[36]

> Whoever is a great poet, the same man is great
> but Spina is a great poet
> therefore Spina is great.
> It is a *sophisma secundum quid et simpliciter,* since it does not
> follow that if 'great' is predicated of Spina along with the determina-
> tion 'poet,' 'great' is also predicated absolutely. For there it is an
> accidental predication, since 'great' is predicated of Spina according
> to an accident. And so it does not follow. It seems however, that this
> word 'great' changes its significance from different adjuncts, since
> when it is said 'Spina is a great poet,' it means 'is great in poetry';
> but when it is said simply 'Spina is great,' it means 'great in body.'
> And according to this it appears that this is a paralogism in the
> third mode of equivocation.

This distinction was commonplace not only in works of academic
logic but also in the day-to-day life of those with any scholastic
training, for it becomes a matter for various types of scholarly jokes.
Jean de Jandun says that to live in Paris is to exist *simpliciter* but
to live anywhere else is only to exist *secundum quid.*[37] A humorous
poem from the *Carmina Burana,* perhaps by Walter of Chatillon,
preaches the Aristotelian idea of liberality as the mean between
prodigality and miserliness, with a reminder that an action may be
good under particular circumstance but not absolutely:

> dare non ut covenit
>   non est a virtute
> bonum est secundum quid
>   sed non absolute;
> digne dare poteris
>   et mereri tute
> famam muneris
> si me prius noveris
>   intus et in cute.[38]

To give inappropriately is not the part of virtue. [To give] is good
conditionally but not absolutely. You can give worthily and safely
deserve the fame of the good deed if you first know me thoroughly.

The *Gawain* poet offers his audience what is, in effect, a pair of interlocking arguments. He says that the pentangle is endless and that Truth is endless and that the pentangle is therefore an appropriate sign for Truth:

> Hit is a syngne þat Salamon set sumquyle
> In bytoknying of trawþe, bi tytle þat hit habbez,
> For hit is a figure þat haldez fyue poyntez,
> And vche lyne vmbelappez and loukez in oþer,
> And ayquere hit is endelez. (626–9)

It is a sign that Solomon once established as a token of *trawþ*, which it has a right to be, because it is a figure that has five points, and each line overlaps and locks into another, and everywhere it is endless.

He says next that the pentangle is a sign for Truth and that Gawain is true, and that the pentangle is therefore an appropriate sign for Gawain:

> Forþy hit acordez to þis knyȝt and to his cler armez,
> For ay faythful in fyue and sere fyue syþez
> Gawan watz for gode knawen, and as golde pured,
> Voyded of vche vylany, wyth vertuez ennourned
>   in mote
>   Forþy þe pentangel nwe
>   He ber in schelde and cote,
>   As tulk of tale most trwe. (631–8)

Therefore it is suited to this knight and to his bright arms, for, always faithful in five ways and five times in each way, Gawain was known as good and, like refined gold, freed of each villainy and adorned with virtues in the field. Therefore he bore the new pentangle on shield and coat, as a man most true of word.

The first of these arguments has already been examined and found to be correct in terms of contemporary ideas about signs and contemporary theorizing about endless signs. The second argument must be examined according to the rules of fallacies, for, as we shall see, a man may be referred to by the same sign as God only *secundum quid*, a fact that is subtly noted by the poet and leads to an important distinction between alternate, context-sensitive meanings of the word *trawþ*.

Even as early as the discussion by Augustine of Psalm 81 there is an important shift in attitude towards those who are called gods and those who will fall like men. Where the text of the psalm itself shows a concern with what they are and with what they will do ('estis,' 'moriemini,' 'cadetis'), Augustine wishes to show that while men may fall through their own unaided effort, they may rise and become gods only by external aid: this is surely the force of the passive verbs describing how one group has been predestined ('qui praedestinati sunt in vitam aeternam') while the other group will not be raised ('non extollemini'). There is also a shift from the original topic for the psalm as a whole; what began as a condemnation of those who passed judgments without respect for true justice has become an attack on the pride of princes, as the full text of Augustine's exegesis of verses 6 and 7 shows:

> Terrenae autem felicitatis regnum superbia est, contra quam venit humilitas Christi, exprobans eis quos vult ex humilitate filios Altissimi facere, atque increpans: *Ego dixi, Dii estis, et filii Altissimi omnes. Vos autem sicut homines moriemini, et sicut unus ex principibus cadetis.* Sive ad illos dixerit, *Ego dixi, Dii estis, et filii Altissimi omnes,* ad eos utique qui praedestinati sunt in vitam aeternam; ad alios vero, *Vos autem sicut homines moriemini, et sicut unus ex principibus cadetis,* hoc modo etiam deos discernens: sive omnes simul increpat, ut obedientes correctos discernat, *Ego,* inquit, *dixi, Dii estis et filii Altissimi omnes;* id est, omnibus vobis promisi coelestem felicitatem; *vos autem,* per infirmitatem carnis, *sicut homines moriemini et,* per elationem animi, *sicut unus ex principibus,* id est diabolus, non extollemini, sed *cadetis.* Velut si diceret: Cum tam pauci sint dies vitae vestrae, ut cito sicut homines moriamini, non vobis prodest ad correctionem; sed tanquam diabolus, cuius dies in hoc saeculo multi sunt, quia carne non moritur, extollimini, ut cadatis. Per diabolicam quippe superbiam factum est, ut Christi gloriae perversi et caeci principes Judaeorum invidissent: per hoc vitium factum est et fit, ut Christi usque ad mortem crucifixi humilitas vilescat eis qui hujus saeculi diligunt excellentiam.[39]

But the kingdom of earthly happiness is pride, to oppose which came the lowliness of Christ, rebuking those whom he wished by lowliness to make the children of the Most High, and blaming them:

'I said, Ye are gods, ye are all the children of the Most High' (v 6),
'But ye shall die like men, and fall like one of the princes' (v 7).
Whether to those he said this, 'I said, Ye are gods,' to those particularly who are predestined to eternal life; and to the others, 'But ye
shall die like men, and shall fall like one of the princes,' in this way
distinguishing the gods; or whether he blames all together, in order
to distinguish the obedient and those who received correction, 'I said,
Ye are gods, and ye are all the children of the Most High:' that is,
to all of you I promised celestial happiness, 'but ye,' through the in-
firmity of your flesh, 'shall die like men,' and through haughtiness
of soul, 'like one of the princes,' that is, the devil, shall not be
exalted, but 'shall fall.' As if he said: 'Though the days of your life
are few, that ye readily die like men, this avails not to your correction: but like the devil, whose days are many in this world, because
he dies not in the flesh, ye are lifted up so that ye fall. For by
devilish pride it came to pass that the perverse and blind rulers of the
Jews envied the glory of Christ: by this vice it came to pass, and
still is, that the lowliness of Christ crucified unto death is lightly
esteemed in the eyes of them who love the excellence of this world.[40]

The circumstances, for Augustine, under which certain men may
become *dii* include that they be predestined to glory and that they
maintain humility throughout their lives in this world; those who
fall are those who place too high a value on worldly matters and
try to exalt themselves.

This admonition, that we must persist in the humility that comes
from true self-knowledge (that is, the knowledge that we are creatures) even when we are being promised divinity, is expressed in
more scholastic form by the author of *The Cloud of Unknowing:*

Abouen þi-self þou arte: for whi þou atteynest to come þedir by grace,
wheþer þou mayst not come by kynde; þat is to sey, to be onyd to
God in spirit & in loue & in acordaunce of wille. Byneþe þi God þou
arte: for whi þof al it may be seide in maner þat in þis tyme God
& þou ben not two bot one in spirit – in so moche þat þou or anoþer
for soche onheed þat feleþ þe perfeccion of þis werk may soþfastly,
bi witnes of Scripture, be clepid a God – neuerþeles зit þou arte
bineþe hym. For whi he is God by kynde wiþ-outen biginnying; &
þou þat sumtyme were nouзt in substaunce & þerto after when
þou were by his miзt & his loue maad ouзt, wilfuly wiþ synne madest
þi-self wors þen nouзt: only bi his mercy wiþ-outen þi desert arte

maad a God in grace, onyd wiþ him in spirit wiþ-outen departyng, boþe here & in blis of heuen wiþ-outen any eende. So þat, þouȝ þou be al one wiþ hym in grace, ȝit þou arte ful fer bineþe hym in kynde.⁴¹

You are above yourself, for you are able to come there by grace where you may not come by nature; that is to say, united with God in spirit and in love and in accord of will. You are beneath your God: because, although it may be said in a manner of speaking that God and you are not two but one in spirit – inasmuch as you or another who truly feels the perfection of this work may, by witness of Scripture, be called a god – nevertheless, you are beneath him. Because he is God without beginning, and you who once were nothing in substance, and afterward, when you were made something by his might and his love, you wilfully and sinfully made yourself worse than nothing. Only by his mercy without deserving it are you made a god in grace, united with him in spirit without any separation, both here and in the bliss of heaven without any end. So that, though you are one with him in grace, yet you are far beneath him in nature.

God is God *simpliciter*, and a man may be called God only *secundum quid*, united with God only 'in maner.' He is not simply 'one' with God; he is 'onyd' with him, 'maad' a god by grace. In the words of Dan Michel in the *Ayenbite of Inwit*:

we ne byeþ naȝt his zones be kende/ bote asemoche þet we byeþ ymad to his anliknesse. ac alsuo byeþ þe sarasyns. ac we byeþ his zones be grace and by adopcion. Adopcioun zuo is a word of laȝe. uor by þe laȝes of þe emperurs/ huanne an heȝ man ne heþ no child: ha may chiese þet child of a guod man yef he wyle. and maki him his zone be adopcioun. þet is be auoerie. zuo þet he ssel bi yhealde uor his zone auoud/ and ssel bere his eritage. Þise grace god ous made þe uader wyþoute oure ofseruinge. ase zayþ saynt pauel. Huanne he ous dede come to þe cristendome we were poure and naked/ and child of yre/ and of helle.⁴²

We are not his sons by nature except inasmuch as we are made in his image, as the Saracens also are, but we are his sons by grace and adoption. Adoption is a word of law, for by the laws of the emperors, when a man has no child he may choose the child of a good man

if he wants to and make him his son by adoption, that is by procla-
mation, so that he will be considered his son and will inherit from
him. God the Father did this grace for us without our deserving it, as
Saint Paul says: 'When he brought us to Christendom we were
poor and naked, children of ire and hell.'

The same kind of construction was put, in the later Middle Ages,
on the requirement from the Gospel of Matthew that men be perfect
as God is perfect. In this case we have the benefit of an authoritative
gloss from the Fourth Lateran Council (1215 AD):

> Cum ergo Veritas pro fidelibus suis ad Patrem orat: volo, inquiens, ut
> ipsi *sint unum in nobis sicut et nos unum sumus* [Io. 17:22], hoc
> nomen, *unum*, pro fidelibus quidem accipitur, ut intelligatur unio
> caritatis in gratia, pro personis vero divinis, ut attendatur identitatis
> in natura unitas, quemadmodum Veritas alibi ait: *Estote perfecti*
> *sicut et Pater vester coelestis perfectus est* [Mt. 5:48], ac si diceret
> manifestius: *Estote perfecti* perfectione gratiae, *sicut et Pater vester*
> *coelestis perfectus est* perfectione naturae, utraque videlicet suo
> modo, quia inter creatorem et creaturam non potest tanta similitudo
> notari, quin inter eos maior sit dissimilitudo notanda.[43]

> As therefore the Truth prays for his faithful to the Father, saying 'I
> wish that they may be one in us just as we are one' (John 17:22), this
> word 'one' is accepted indeed for the faithful as if to mean the
> union of charity in grace, but for the divine persons as if the unity of
> identity in nature is meant, just as the Truth says elsewhere 'Be
> you therefore perfect, as also your heavenly Father is perfect' (Matt
> 5:48), but if he spoke more openly, 'Be you therefore perfect' by
> perfection of grace, 'as also your heavenly Father is perfect' by perfec-
> tion of nature, each clearly in his own manner, since it cannot be
> that so much similarity is noted between creator and creature that
> greater dissimilarity is not to be noted between them.

Aquinas's gloss on this passage from Matthew shows a similar
concern for the differences in the types of perfection possible for God
and men:

> *sicut et pater vester caelestis perfectus est.* Glossa: '*Sicut* imitationem
> notat, non aequalitatem'; quasi dicat: Hoc quod dixi faciatis, ut
> mereamini esse filii patris caelestis per adoptionis gratiam.[44]

'as also your heavenly Father is perfect.' Gloss: '*Sicut* denotes imitation, not equality,' as if he says: Do this which I have said, so that you may deserve to be the sons of the heavenly Father through the grace of adoption.

These explanations of the biblical texts make it clear that it is possible for the same name or sign to be applied to both God and man, but only *secundum quid*. Man may be called God or a son of God not because his entire nature corresponds to divine nature but only because of a certain limited correspondence between their natures. Further, if a man is called God, it is not the automatic result of our creation in God's image but is brought about through the agency of divine grace. The pentangle as a sign for God can therefore also signify a man only if he is in a state of grace and only by transference.

D   THE EFFECT OF SIGNS ON THEIR AUDIENCE

I   Heraldic and Religious Signs

When the heraldic theorists wished to decide whether it was legitimate for one man to bear another's arms, they did not, as we have seen, restrict their analysis to purely semantic considerations. Instead, the manuals moved to another level of meaning and considered the effect of the use of the sign on an audience; if the bearer wears the arms in a shameful manner or in such a way as to deceive or defraud others, then the original owner has legitimate grounds for complaint. The full meaning of the act of wearing arms can only be understood, therefore, through a knowledge of the effect it has on other people.

These same distinctions must be made in the case of certain coats of arms that, though they identify particular men or particular families, take their form not from the qualities of the bearer but from a claim or vow that he makes. The Douglas family armour, for example, includes a human heart, not because of any hidden canting significance or any reference to personal qualities, but rather, 'the heart in the arms of Douglas alludes to the vow of Sir James Douglas to take the heart of Bruce to the Holy Land.'[45] Similarly, though such devices as the crosses on the armour of a man named Cross and even the phoenix on the crest of a man named Christie[46] may have an etymological purpose, the cross on a crusader's arms must be seen as a statement or confession of belief by the bearer rather than as a simple bodying-forth of his attributes. Such devices must be understood not only in semantic terms but in accordance with their evocative powers.

Divine heraldic signs, when ascribed to divine beings, have a purely semantic function, but when they are connected with humans, their effect becomes as important as their signification. There is a monumental brass of John of Campden, who died in 1382, showing him flanked by the Arms of Christ and the Arms of the Trinity (see Figure 5).[47] In this case, however, the armour does not signify the bearer, nor does it simply signify Christ and the Trinity. The devices are instead visible statements of the objects of John's belief, comparable to the inscriptions on the brass, 'Credo quod redemptor meus vivit' and 'In novissimo die de terra surrecturus sum et rursum circumdabor pelle mea et in carne meo videbo deum salvatorem meum.' Rodney Dennys quotes a poem from a late fourteenth-century manuscript that describes the Arms of Christ and gives a comparable explanation of the circumstance for their use:

> A scheld of red, a crosse of grene,
> A crown ywrithe with thornes kene,
> A spere, a spounge, with nayles thre,
> A body ybounde to a tre,
> Who so this scheld in hert wyl take,
> Among hys enemyes thahre he not quake.[48]

> A shield of red, a cross of green, a crown wreathed with sharp thorns, a spear, a sponge, with three nails, a body bound to a tree – whoever will take this shield into his heart will not quake among his enemies.

Such thinking is evident also in the fact that both Richard Rolle and Henry Suso are depicted with the monogram of Christ carved on their chests.[49]

The instruments of Christ's passion are further treated, one by one and in a non-heraldic context, as aids to reformation and the contemplation of Christian truths, in another fourteenth-century poem, *The Symbols of the Passion*. After a pictorial illustration of each symbol, including the vernicle, the knife of circumcision, and the pelican, as well as the actual instruments of the passion, the poet presents a verbal description and a brief petition that the symbol may have a beneficial effect on us: the rods are a help against sloth; the

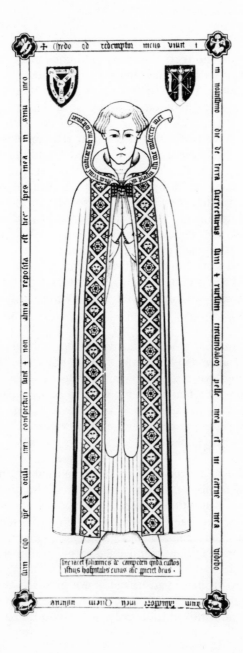

Figure 5   Monumental brass of John of Campden

crown of thorns is a shield against hell; the nails help us out of
sins of the hands and feet; the spear quenches pride.[50]

Heraldic signs with particularly religious messages and signs
representing moments in Christian history are therefore only a part
of a complex of ideas about the purpose and meaning of various
types of religious images. It is not only that the particular pictures
are thought to have particular effects but that images in general owe
their utility to their power to influence their audience for their
good. This concern is displayed on the theoretical level by Nicholas
of Cusa, who does not simply describe his infinite geometrical
figures and claim that they are signs for God but argues in addition
that they aid human imagination in moving towards a deeper
knowledge of God.[51] Further, when the English Lollards accused the
Church of violating the first commandment by venerating images,
the orthodox response relied on the salutary powers of images in
order to defend the practice. Basing their views on the arguments of
early Fathers such as Gregory and John Damascene,[52] orthodox
defenders of images asserted that

> þey ben ordeynd to steryn manys mende to thynkyn of Cristys
> incarnacioun and of his passioun and of holye seyntys lyuys. Also
> þey been ordeynyd to steryn mannys affeccioun and his herte to
> deuocioun, for often man is more steryd be syght þan be heryng or
> redyngge. Also þey been ordeynyd to been a tokene and a book to
> þe lewyd peple, þat þey moun redyn in ymagerye and peynture þat
> clerkys redyn in boke.[53]

> They are ordained to stir men's minds to think of Christ's incarnation
> and passion and of the lives of holy saints. Also they are ordained
> to stir man's affection and heart to devotion, for often man is more
> stirred by sight than by hearing or reading. Also they are ordained to
> be a token and a book to ignorant people, so that they may read in
> imagery and painting what learned people read in books.

The honour shown before an image is not given to the image itself,
but to the being of which it is a sign. Images used in this way are
not forbidden, and indeed their cultivation should be seen as a positive duty:

> Non ergo semper cultus imaginum provocat ad idolatriam, sed magis,
> ubi est regimen intellectus, ad cultum unius Dei, qui tales habet

famulos spiritus excellentes; qualiter sanctus Enos intelligitur fecisse,
& coluisse imagines in honorem Dei ad deprimendum idolatriam,
per falsum cultum daemonum imaginibus praestitum a filiis Cain,
secundum quod Nicolaus exponit.[54]

For the cult of images does not always provoke to idolatry but rather,
where there is control of the intellect, to the cult of the one God,
who has such servants, excellent of spirit; just as holy Enoch is
understood to have made images and practised their cult to the
honour of God, in order to suppress idolatry, as expressed in the false
cult of demons performed with images by the children of Cain,
according to what Nicholas expounds.

2   The Shield of Faith

Of those devices appropriated for human use from the realm of
divine heraldry, the one that offers the greatest possibilities for comparison to Gawain's pentangle is the Arms of the Trinity, the inter-
twined set of statements about the relationship between the three
persons of God. Like the pentangle, it can be discussed *in vacuo* as
an interlocking, endless, and apparently paradoxical geometrical figure whose meaning accords with its visible qualities. But since it
was also used as an heraldic device, its full meaning can be determined only through a fuller consideration of the circumstances of its
use. When it is ascribed to God, or Christ, or to the Trinity as a
whole, the special properties of the heraldic system are simply being
used to meet a felt need in medieval culture: 'The pictorial language
of heraldry was ideally suited to making abstract powers manifest.
The Biblical prohibition against making images of God could easily
be circumvented by representing the elusive concept of the Holy
Trinity symbolically.'[55] But this shield is attributed to other bearers
as well. Tremlett, in his edition of the Matthew Paris Shields,
reports that the device was assigned to St Michael, and it may also
be found in the arms of a bishop of York and of Christ Church,
London. Finally, an illustration in the *Lambeth Apocalypse* (see
Frontispiece) shows a young woman defending herself against the
arrows of the devil with a shield bearing the device, this time lettered
in French.[56]

Now, when such a shield is considered to be the armour of God,
the relationship between sign and bearer is nothing more than pure
signification. The qualities of the bearer are manifested in a sche-

matic representation. But when it is ascribed to a particular human or to a church, the sign's relationship to its owner must be of a different order. A bishop who uses a set of interlocking propositions about the nature of the Trinity as his own personal device is not claiming to *be* the Trinity or to possess its qualities but is rather confessing his belief in the Trinity and acknowledging his reliance on the truths the device expresses. He has a right to the arms by reason of the sacrament of ordination. Similarly, the young woman in the illumination who uses the Arms of the Trinity as a defence against evil is not making a claim about her own nature but is rather showing her faith in the truth of the Trinity to protect herself. Her title to the device is also sacramental, but in this case it is the sacrament of penance. As the writing on the illustration declares, 'par la Dame est signifié repentent,' and 'par l'escu, la fei.'

This last equation, between the shield and faith, associates the device with a well-known passage from St Paul. He exhorts the Christian to arm himself against temptations, saying

> Propterea accipite armaturam Dei, ut possitis resistere in die malo, et in omnibus perfecti stare. State ergo succincti lumbos vestros in veritate, et induti loricam iustitiae, et calceati pedes in praeparatione Evangelii pacis: in omnibus sumentes scutum fidei, in quo possitis omnia tela nequissimi ignea extinguere: et galeam salutis assumite: et gladium spiritus (quod est verbum Dei). (Eph 6:13–17)

> Therefore take unto you the armour of God, that you may be able to resist in the evil day, and to stand in all things perfect. Stand therefore, having your loins girt about with truth, and having on the breastplate of justice, And your feet shod with the preparation of the gospel of peace: In all things taking the shield of faith, wherewith you may be able to extinguish all the fiery darts of the most wicked one. And take unto you the helmet of salvation, and the sword of the Spirit (which is the word of God).

Contemporary commentators take pains to show that the Shield of Faith, however it is visually conceived, is not simply a signifying device but is rather something that communicates and that stirs the mind of the beholder, whether the bearer or another. Robert Holkott, in his *Super Libros Sapientiae*, describes the shield of King Arthur and then explains the way in which his *exemplum* applies to his own audience:

In hystoria britonum scribitur de Archturo rege quod in interiori
parte scuti sui imaginem virginis gloriose depictam habuit quam
quotiens in bello fatigatus aspexit spem recuperavit et vires. Isto
modo nos si in bello vite presentis triumphare velimus, infra scutum
fidei nostre imaginem virginis cum filio deportemus. Hanc respicia-
mus et in ea confidamus quia ab ea vires et virtutes recipiemus.
Ambrosius de sancta virginitate. Sit nobis tanquam in imagine depicta
vita Marie ex qua velut ex speculo refulget spes castitatis et forma
virtutis.[57]

In the *History of the Britons* it is written about King Arthur that he
had an image of the glorious Virgin painted on the interior of his
shield, and that whenever he was tired in battle and looked at it, he
recovered his hope and force. In this manner, if we wish to be
triumphant in this present life, let us carry an image of the Virgin
with her Son under the shield of our faith. Let us look at her and
trust in her since we receive force and virtues from her. Ambrose
says in *De Sancta Virginitate*, 'Let the life of Mary be, as it were,
painted for us in a picture from which as from a mirror the hope
of chastity and the form of virtue may reflect.'

The general currency of both his image and this interpretation may
be seen from the fact that it is quoted, with minor variations and
no reference to Holkott, by Thomas Brinton[58] and by the author of a
contemporary English sermon:

I rede in Gestis Britonum, et recitat doctor Holcote super Librum
Sapiencie, þat Kyng Artoure had in þe innare parte of ys shelde and
ymage of Oure Lady Mary deprented, berying a child in her armes,
þe wiche ymage he wold behold when that he was werry in batell and
feynte; and anon for conforte and hope þat he had in hure he waxed
freshe and herty aȝeyn and in als good poynte for to feyȝthe as he
was at þe begynnyng. Ryght so in þe same wyze þou þat arte in batell
here on erthe and fyȝthynge not only aȝeyns bodely enmyes but also
aȝeyns goostely, þat is þe world, þe feend, and þin own fleshe, þerfor loke þat þou haue Marye, Goddis modur, in þe innare parte of þi
sheld, þat is þi feyȝth and þin beleve. Sett þat only vppon hure.
Þan trewly she will not forsake þe.[59]

I read in *The Deeds of the Britons*, and doctor Holcot says in his
book on Wisdom, that King Arthur had an image of our Lady Mary,

with a child in her arms, painted on the inside of his shield, and
he would look at this image when he was weary and faint in battle.
At once, for the comfort and the hope that he had in her, he became
fresh and hearty again and as ready and able to fight again as he
was at the beginning. In exactly the same way, you who are in a
battle here on earth and fighting not only against bodily enemies but
also against spiritual enemies, that is, the world, the devil, and
your own flesh, therefore, take care that you have Mary, God's
mother, on the inside of your shield, that is, your faith and your
belief. Set that only upon her. Then truly she will not forsake you.

It is not only the pictures painted on the inside of the Shield of Faith
that are described in such terms, for the external device is also
presented as serving the purpose of preserving and increasing spiritual
fortitude:

> Also he byddith us takyn to us þe scheld of feith, for as þe scheld is a
> triangle and hath þre cornerys, in whyche triangle ȝif from þe myddis
> ben drawyn þre lyneys into þe þre cornerys þer schul ben þre triang-
> lys, whyche þre arn but on triangle, & þou non of hem is oþir.
> And þerfor þe feith of þe holy trinite is lykenyd to a scheld, for þer
> ben þre personys in þe holy trinite – þe fadir & þe sone and þe
> holy gost, & iche of hem is God and non of hem is oþir & þouȝ ben
> þey alle þre but on God in maieste. This scheld of feith of þe holy
> trinite us must takyn to us in gostly fyȝt and leuyn in þe holy trinite
> & settyn al our feith and al our trost in on God in trinite and
> preyyn to þe fadir almyȝty þat he sende us myȝt, to þe sone al witty
> þat he grante us wit and wisdam, to þe holy gost al gracious & ful
> of mercy þat he grante us grace, so þat we mon han myȝt, wit and
> grace to withstondyn alle gostly enmyys.[60]

> Also he bids us take unto ourselves the Shield of Faith, for just as
> the shield is a triangle and has three corners, in which, if three lines
> are drawn from the centre into the three corners, there will be
> three triangles, yet these three are but one triangle, and no one of
> them is the other. And therefore the faith of the Holy Trinity is
> compared to a shield, for there are three persons in the Holy Trinity
> – the Father and the Son and the Holy Ghost, and each of them is
> God and none of them is the other and though they are three they are
> but one God in power. This Shield of Faith of the Holy Trinity we
> must take to ourselves in spiritual fight and believe in the Holy

Trinity and set all our faith and all our trust in one God in Trinity
and pray to the almighty Father that he send us might, to the all-wise
Son that he send us wit and wisdom, to the all-gracious Holy Ghost,
full of mercy, that he grant us grace, so that we may have might,
wit, and grace to withstand all spiritual enemies.

These descriptions of the Shield of Faith show that a fourteenth-
century audience, hearing about a shield with an endless, interlocking design representing Truth on the outside and having a picture
of the Virgin on the inside, could be expected to recognize that the
bearer was at that moment considered to be in circumstances that
would allow him to be signified by a sign for God, that he was declaring to the world his faith in God, and that he was conscious of
his need for aid from an external, divine source for his continued
well-being.

3 Faith and Truth

We have seen in the discussion about the problem of deification in the previous chapter that it is necessary for there to be an action of divine grace in order for a human to be referred to by a sign that ordinarily stands for God. The author of *The Cloud of Unknowing*, even as he is promising deification, reminds us that we 'come þedir by grace,' and the Fourth Lateran Council explanation for 'be ye perfect' insists on the addition 'by perfection of grace.'[1] It is only to be expected, therefore, that a poet working in fourteenth-century England would share the presuppositions about the necessity for grace that were so central to medieval Christianity. But as the previous section has shown, we do not need to rely on general similiarities or even on assumptions of shared belief when we are dealing with a poet as careful with words as the *Gawain* poet proves to be, for he always provides us with the necessary material for testing such hypotheses. A close examination of the details of the verbal nuances in the pentangle passage allows us to see that Gawain's title to his shield is also, in a certain measure, conditional and not absolute, based on his being in a state of grace.

Just as the choice of verb forms and the type of language used by Augustine and the *Cloud* author in their exposition of Psalm 81 was an indication of an orientation different from a reading without presuppositions about the necessity for divine grace, so too there are hints in the pentangle passage that Gawain's *trawþ* is his only through the agency of an external power. It is not only the direct statements that his 'forsnes' is derived from the five joys of Mary or that he placed his trust in Christ's wounds that suggest the importance of the larger context, but also the ways in which the qualities ascribed to him are bracketed and set off to prevent them from being seen as natural perfections. Indeed, there is considerable possibility for doubt in this passage, since there is only one unequivocal statement about these qualities, that he 'fayled never' (641); this is contradicted, of course, by the further progress of the narrative. But while this failure has been examined elsewhere in detail, too little attention has been paid to the implications of the fact that the poet uses equivocal or ambiguous terms in the other statements.

The first group of such statements is comprised of those hinting that Gawain's perfection is merely apparent – that is, of lines that, when taken strictly, assert only that he seemed to be perfect. Among these are included the statements that 'Gawan watz for gode *knawen*' (633), that he was 'tulk *of tale* most trwe' (638), and that he was '*Funden* fautlez' (640). There is nothing here to suggest that Gawain was in reality vicious, and nothing comparable to Chaucerian irony. In fact each of the descriptions is open to a highly positive interpretation. To say that a man is 'known' to be good is certainly stronger than merely to say that he was 'thought' to be good. The phrase 'of tale' could be construed as relating to Gawain's own speech rather than that of other people, and be taken to mean that he was true in his speech, not that he was reputed to be true. It is possible to read 'funden' in the light of OED *find* 6: 'To discover, come to knowledge of (a fact or a state of things) by experience or trial,' and so to conclude that Gawain is both 'tried and true.' But the difficulty remains that these are not completely unequivocal statements of his worth. The various terms are, in effect, bracketed and in a different category from natural and permanent attributes.

The second group consists of passive participles used to describe Gawain, which have the same effect as the passive verbs used by St Augustine. Gawain is not said to be 'void' of villainy but 'voyded,' and he is 'ennourned' with virtues (634). Though the pentangle itself is made of 'pure' gold (620), Gawain is compared with 'pured' gold (633). Taken together, these separate touches are an indication that the passage should be read taking into account the doctrine that God is the source of all human virtues. This is true not only for ordinary humans, but even for the Virgin herself. The twelve stars of her crown represent the virtues, and the roundness of the crown represents their perfection; but the virtues are not hers by nature, since they are given to her by grace, just as the stars receive their light from the sun. The difference between the Virgin and other humans is that the perfection of her virtue is dependent upon receiving grace wholly rather than in parts:

> And Seynt Ierom in Epistola ad Paulam et Eustachium rememburs of þis plentevous grace ȝeuen to þis Ladie, writyng þus, 'Gracia ceteris per partes prestatur; Marie autem tota se infudit plenitudo gracie' – grace was ȝeue to oþure by partes, but to Oure Ladie þe plente of grace was held on hure alle hole.[2]

> Saint Jerome, in his letter to Paul and Eustachius, mentions this complete grace given to our lady, saying, 'Grace was given to others partially, but to our lady the plenitude of grace was given completely.'

If Gawain has a title to a shield bearing a sign of divine perfection, it is the same type of title as that of the young woman in the *Lambeth Apocalypse* – a sacramental title. The shield is his only conditionally, only so long as he remains in a state of grace.

B   FAITH AND TRUTH

I   The Meaning of *Trawþ*

The next stage of the process of definition of the meaning-in-context of the pentangle depends on the logicians' ideas of *suppositio* and *equivocatio*. We have already seen one example of this concern in the syllogism about the poet Spina. Depending on the other words in the proposition, the word *great* may stand for the idea 'great in poetry' or else 'great in body.' This standing-for is what the logicians called *suppositio*. In this case it is closely connected with the idea of *equivocatio*, discussed above in connection with the heraldic devices borne by more than one man. In addition to terms such as personal names, which are equivocal by chance, some terms are said to be intentionally equivocal:

> Aliud est aequivocum a consilio, quando vox primo imponitur alicui vel aliquibus et subordinatur uni conceptui, et postea propter aliquam similitudinem primi significati ad alquid aliud vel propter aliquam aliam rationem imponitur illi alteri, ita quod non imponeretur illi alteri, nisi quia primo imponebatur alii, sicut est de hoc nomine 'homo'; primo enim imponebatur ad significandum omnia animalia rationalia, ita quod imponebatur ad significandum omne illud, quod

continetur sub hoc conceptu, 'animal rationale,' postea autem
utentes videntes similitudinem inter talem hominem et imaginem
hominis, utebantur quandoque hoc nomine 'homo' pro tali imagine,
ita quod, nisi hoc nomen 'homo' fuisset primo impositum homini-
bus, non uterentur nec imponerent hoc nomen 'homo' ad significandum vel standum pro tali imagine; et propter hoc dicitur
'aequivocum a consilio.'[3]

But equivocality can also be intentional. Here, a word is first assigned
to one thing or several things and is, thus, subordinated to one
concept. But, afterwards, because the things signified by the term are
similar to or bear some other relation to other things, the term is
used to signify something new. Its new use, however, is not merely
accidental. If it had not been assigned to items of the first sort it
would not be used in the second case. An example is the term 'man.'
In the first instance, this term is used to signify all rational animals,
so that it is imposed to signify all those things which are subsumed
under the concept *rational animal*. But afterwards, those using
the term see a similarity between men and their images in pictures.
Thus, they use the term 'man' to signify the pictorial representations
of men, but notice that they would not use the term 'man' to
signify or stand for the representations of men unless they had first
used the word in the case of real men. For this reason we say that
'man' is equivocal by intention.[4]

It is the propositional context that allows us to determine which
of the alternate meanings is appropriate. The word *currit*, to take
a common example, means 'runs' when applied to animals but 'flows'
when applied to rivers, so that we are able to define what is fallacious about such syllogisms as:

> *quicquid currit, habet pedes*
> *Secana currit*
> *ergo Secana habet pedes.*[5]

> Whatever runs, has feet.
> The Seine runs.
> Therefore the Seine has feet.

This distinction allows us to formulate another hypothesis concerning the attribution of the pentangle to two different referents. Such

a procedure would have been seen as legitimate and unproblematic, provided that proper attention was paid to the propositional context in which the sign was used. Just as the possible meanings of *runs* and *man* are limited and defined by the nature of the other terms in the proposition, so too the choices of meaning of the pentangle are are defined by the nature of the being of whom it is 'predicated.' Analysis of the functioning of this equivocation is quite straightforward: after determining the two possible significations and understanding the reasons for the differences between them, we can proceed to the underlying *similitudo* or *aliqua alia ratio* that led to the intentional application of the term to referents other than its original concept.

Veritas is treated as just such an equivocal term, because of the fact that it is used in both absolute and relative senses. Anselm's description of *Summa Veritas*, discussed above, includes a forceful statement about the difference between absolute *veritas* and the *veritas* of a particular thing, arguing that it is so great that to speak of 'the truth of this thing or that' is to speak very loosely:

> Improprie 'huius vel illius rei' esse dicitur, quoniam illa non in ipsis rebus aut ex ipsis aut per ipsos in quibus esse dicitur habet suum esse. Sed cum res ipsae secundum illam sunt, quae semper praesto est iis quae sunt sicut debent: tunc dicitur 'huius vel illius rei veritas,' ut veritas voluntatis, actionis, quemadmodum dicitur 'tempus huius vel illius rei,' cum unum et idem sit tempus omnium quae in eodem tempore simul sunt; et si non esset haec vel illa res, non minus esset idem tempus. Non enim ideo dicitur tempus huius vel illius rei, quia tempus est in ipsis rebus, sed quia ipsae sunt in tempore. Et sicut tempus per se consideratum non dicitur tempus alicuius, sed cum res quae in illo sunt consideramus, dicimus 'tempus huius vel illius rei': ita summa veritas per se subsistens nullius rei est; sed cum aliquid secundum illam est, tunc eius dicitur veritas vel rectitudo.[6]

> We speak improperly when we say 'the truth of this thing' or 'the truth of that thing.' For truth does not have its being *in* or *from* or *through* the things in which it is said to be. But when these things are in accordance with truth, which is always present to things which are as they ought to be, then we say 'the truth of that thing' (for example, 'the truth of the will' or 'the truth of action'). Similarly, we say 'the time of this thing' or 'the time of that thing,' although

there is one and the same time for all things which exist together at the same time. And if *this* thing did not exist, or if *that* thing did not exist, time would nonetheless remain the same; for we say 'the time of this thing' or 'the time of that thing' not because time is in these things but because these things are in time. Now, when considered in itself, time is not called the time of anything; but when we consider things which are in time, we say 'the time of this thing' or 'the time of that thing.' Similarly, Supreme Truth, existing in and of itself, is not the truth of anything; but when something accords with Supreme Truth, then we speak of the truth or rightness of that thing.[7]

These distinctions therefore allow for greater precision in our discussion of the meaning of Gawain's pentangle. If we call him 'true,' or speak about 'his truth,' or ascribe to him as armour a sign for absolute truth, we are speaking loosely, and what we actually mean is that he is, at that point in time, *in accord with* truth.

The usual name for the quality a man displays when he is in this state is faith. When Gawain wears the Shield of Faith, he is not doing so simply for its evocative and communicative powers. In addition to declaring that Gawain trusts in the truth and in addition to instructing observers in the nature of truth, the shield labels Gawain as true in a relative sense, that is, faithful. In a proposition about God, either truth or the pentangle may be *per se consideratum*; but in a proposition concerning Gawain they are restricted in meaning and declare not that truth exists in Gawain but that Gawain exists in truth.

Fortunately, in the dialect of the *Gawain* poet the same verbal sign may be used for both *veritas* and *fides*, so there is no contradiction in using one visual sign, the pentangle, to stand for both. In addition to its absolute meaning *trawþ* also had relative senses in the fourteenth century: OED 3a, 'Faith, trust, confidence,' and OED 9b, 'Conduct in accordance with the divine standard.' Preachers in this period use *trawþ* to stand for *fides* when they are contrasting faith and works. Dan John Gatryge, for example, offers this definition:

> Þe firste vertu es 'trouthe,' wharethrughe we trow anely in Godd þat made all thynges, with all þe oþer vertus I touchede be-fore. And þis es nedfull till all þat cristenly lyffes; For trouthe es begynnynge

of all gude dedis; For noþer es trouthe worthe with-owtten·gud werk,
ne na werke with-owtten trouthe may pay Godd Almyghty.[8]

The first virtue is *trawþ*, through which we believe only in God who
made all things, with all the other virtues I mentioned before. And
this is necessary for all who live in a Christian way, for *trawþ* is
the beginning of all good deeds. For *trawþ* does not exist without
good works, and no work without *trawþ* may please almighty God.

The Middle English translation of *St Edmund's Mirror* says that the
words 'Qui es' in the paternoster are an indiction of 'trouthe,' that
is, of faith:

Stabill trouthe est takyn in þise wordes *Qui es*; For when we say *qui
es*, þan graunt we wele þat Godd es þat we neuer sawe; and þat es
ryghte trouthe, For trouthe es na noþer thyng bot trowyng of thyng
þat may noghte be sene.[9]

Stable *trawþ* is implied in these words, 'who art,' for when we say
'who art,' then we are granting that God, whom we never saw, exists,
and that is surely *trawþ*, for *trawþ* is nothing but the belief in a
thing that may not be seen.

Richard Rolle translates St Paul's 'per fidem enim ambulamus, et
non per speciem' (II Cor 5:7) as 'we go by trouthe, noghte by syghte,
þat es, we lyff in trouthe, not in bodily felynge'; 'we go by *trawþ*,
not by sight, that is, we live in *trawþ*, not in bodily feeling.'[10] All
four texts of the *Cursor Mundi* gloss Luke's 'Fides tua te salvam
fecit' (Luke 7:50) as 'þi mikel treuth has þe saued'; 'thy great *trawþ*
has saved thee.'[11] A metrical paraphrase of the paternoster connects
this use of the word with the image of a shield:

And ȝefe us mihte þurh his held.
þet ure leue beo ure sceld
aȝein þes fondes fondunge.
þurh trowþe and þurh swicunge.
and he us ȝeue streinde and mihte.
and ȝeue us wepne for to boren.
Mid gode werkes for us to weren.
þet is þurh trouðe. and þurh cherite.[12]

And give us the power, through his grace, that our belief should be
our shield against the deception of this fiend, through faith and toil ...
and may he give us strength and might and give us a weapon to
bear in order to defend ourselves with good works, that is, through
trawþ and through charity.

It is not necessary, and would not be productive, for us simply to
choose between the two meanings, faith and truth, for the pentangle
or for the word *trawþ*, especially since there is strong evidence of
a concern in the period with the relationship between the two qualities. Langland, for example, make a fairly straightforward statement
on the topic through the speeches of Lady Holy Church in Passus
1 of *Piers Plowman*. In her explanation of the Tower, she says,

'The tour on þe toft,' quod she, 'truþe is þerInne,
and wolde þat ye wrouȝte as his word techeþ.
For he is fader of feiþ, and formed yow alle
Both with fel and with face, and yaf you fyue wittes
For to worshippe hym þerwiþ while ye ben here.'

'The tower on the hill,' she said, '*trawþ* is in it, and wishes you to
work as his word teaches. For he is the father of faith, and created you
all, with a body and a face and five senses with which to worship
him while you are here.'

This is Truth as absolute, as a name for God; but seventy lines later
the word is used to refer to a human quality:

Whan alle tresors arn tried treuþe is þe best;
I do it on *Deus caritas* to deme þe soþe.
It is as dereworþe a drury as deere god hymseluen.
[For] who is trewe of his tonge, telleþ noon ooþer,
Dooþ þe werkes þerwiþ and wilneþ no man ille,
He is a god by þe gospel, a grounde and o lofte,
And [ek] ylik to oure lord by Seint Lukes worde.[13]

When all treasures are tested, *trawþ* is the best. To test the truth, I
use the words 'God is love.' It is as precious a jewel as dear God
himself. For he who is true of his tongue, and never says anything

else, who does the works of truth and wills no man ill, he is a god by the gospel, on earth and in heaven, and like our lord, according to Saint Luke's words.

Both the contrast between the two qualities and their intrinsic relationship are well described by D. Murtaugh: ' "Truth" now does not seem to mean "God" but something else as valuable "as deere god hymseluen." It is no longer transcendent, but is in each man who "is trewe of his tonge" and lives a moral life. But the term cannot be transferred to the immanent without bringing some of its transcendent character with it, so that the "trewe" man becomes "a god by þe gospel a ground and o lofte." His good works resound in heaven because they are the expression of Truth, at once the principle of moral action and heaven's king.'[14] This same spirit is at work in the passages from *Pearl* and *Purity* that use the endless roundness of the pearl as a symbol for Christ, for the kingdom of heaven, and for the purity for which each Christian must strive.

2   The Contingency of Human Trawþ

The most striking difference between what Murtaugh calls 'transcendent' and 'immanent' truth is that the former is without beginning or end whereas the latter exists only if it has been brought into being and may be easily terminated by an act of human will. The examples discussed above in connection with the question of deification show that man may be made perfect only by grace. His condition of *trawþ* has a beginning, as does his very being, and it may be ended at any time by a sinful thought or action, as each man recapitulates the original disobedience. As the *Cloud* author reminds us, 'when þou were by his miȝt & his loue maad ouȝt, wilfuly wiþ synne madest þi-self wors þen nouȝt.'[15] This fact is essential to an understanding of the place in the world of even the most upright of men:

> & þerfore þenk on God as in þis werk þou dost on þi-self, & on þi-self as þou dost on God, þat he is as he is & þou arte as þou arte, so þat þi þouȝt be not scaterid ne departid, bot onid in him þat is al; euermore sauyng þis difference betwix þee & him, þat he is þi being & þou not his. For þof it be so þat alle þinges ben in hym bi cause & bi being & he be in alle þinges here cause & here being, ȝit in himself only he is his owne cause & his owne being.[16]

And therefore think on God as you do on yourself in this work, and on yourself as you do on God, that he is as he is and you are as you are, so that your thought will not be scattered or partial but united in him who is all; always saving this difference between you and him, that he is your being and you are not his. For though it may be that things are in him by cause and by being, and he is in all things their cause and their being, yet in himself only he is his own cause and his own being.

Human *trawþ* has a beginning because man is a creature; it has an ending as a result of its composite and relative nature, its existence in a transitory world, and its dependence on a fallen will. Before their death and judgment, even the elect are 'true' only *secundum quid*.

The importance of this distinction, and the meaning of the *Gawain* poet's decision to describe the pentangle as a composite as well as endless figure, may be seen in the contrast between two comparable images from his general tradition. In his discussion of the fifth commandment, the author of *Dives and Pauper* quotes St Augustine to the effect that all ten commandments may be summed up in one precept, and uses a memorable image to show how this accords with the claim by St James (James 2:10–11) that the man who breaks one law breaks all:

And þerfor Sent Iamys seith in his pystyl þat þouȝ a man kepe alle þe lawe & he offende in on he is gylty of alle, for why, seith he, God þat bad þe don no lecherie he bad þe nout slen, and þerfor, seith he, alþei þou do no lecherye & þu sle þu brekyst þe lawe ... And so, as Sent Austyn seith þere, al þe lawe is conteynyd in þis on precept of kende: þat þu wil nout be don to þe, do þu it to non oþir; & so nedys he þat offendyth in on he offendith in alle. And þerfor Dauid & Sent Austyn also clepith Godis lawe a sauterye & an harpe of ten cordis. And þerfor Dauyd byddyth us preysyn God in þe harpe & in þe sauterye of ten cordis, þat is to seye, in þe goode kepyng of þe ten comandementis: Confitemini domino in cithara, in psalterio decem cordarum psallite illi [Ps. 32:2]. And ȝif it be so þat on corde in þe sauterie or in þe harpe be brokyn or out [of] toon or out of acord with oþir cordis, alle þe song þat is pleyyd þerynne schal ben vnlykyng to alle þo þat heryn it & nout plesant.

Therefore, Saint James says in his epistle that though a man keep all the law, if he offends in one he has transgressed all, because, he says, God who commanded you to do no lechery also commanded you not to slay, and so, he says, although you do no lechery, if you slay you break the law ... And so, as Saint Augustine says there, all the law is contained in this one precept of nature: that which you do not want to be done to you, do not do it to another; and so it must be that he that offends in one offends in all. Therefore David and also Saint Augustine call God's law a psaltery and a harp of ten strings. Therefore David bids us praise God with the harp and the psaltery of ten strings, that is to say, in the good keeping of the ten commandments: 'Confess to the lord on the harp, sing to him on the psaltery of ten strings.' And if it be that one string on the psaltery or the harp is broken or out of tune with the other strings, all the song that is played on it will be unpleasant to all who hear it.

After a detailed explanation of how the sin of manslaughter, for example, could be seen as a violation of each of the other separate commandments in turn, he gives an exegesis of the beast of the Apocalypse, making the same general point:

This beste hadde seuene hefdys & ten hornys, þat is to seye, seuene dedly synnys & brekynge of þe ten comandementis, in tokene þat whan man or woman fallith in ony dedly synne opynlyche he fallit in alle seuene pryueliche in Godis syȝthe, & whan he brekyt on com- andement he brekyt alle; & þerfor seith sent Iamys þat he þet offendith in on he offendith in alle & is gilty of alle, Iac. ii |10|.[17]

This beast had seven heads and ten horns, that is to say, seven deadly sins and the breaking of the ten commandments, as a sign that when a man or woman falls openly in any deadly sin, he falls in all seven privately in God's sight, and when he breaks one command- ment he breaks all. Therefore Saint James says that he who offends in one offends in all and is guilty of all.

As long as a man is capable of committing one of the seven deadly sins, as long as he is capable of breaking one of the ten command- ments – that is, as long as he is alive – he is capable of putting an end to his state of being in accord with Truth, an end to his faith:

Therefore, al the while that a man hath in hym the peyne of concu- piscence, it is impossible but he be tempted sometime and moeved in his flessh to synne. And this thyng may nat faille as longe as he lyveth; it may wel wexe fieble and faille by vertu of baptesme, and by the grace of God thurgh penitence; but fully ne shal it nevere quenche ... And therefore seith Seint John the Evaungelist: 'If that we seyn that we be withoute synne, we deceyve us selve, and trouthe is nat in us.'[18]

Therefore, as long as a man has in him the pain of concupiscence, it is impossible that he not be tempted some time, and moved in the flesh to sin. And this may not stop as long as he lives; it may well become weak, and falter through baptism, and by the grace of God through penitence, but it will never completely die out ... And therefore Saint John the evangelist says, 'If we say that we are without sin, we deceive ourselves, and *trawþ* is not in us.'

The *Dives and Pauper* author is also the source of a different image to show the opposite side of the case, an endless and non-composite visual sign to display the permanence of the *trawþ* of the elect. His rich man asks a rather naïve question about portraits with haloes and receives an answer that points up the differences between ordinary live human beings and the saints of heaven:

DIUES Qhat betokenyn þe rounde thynggys þat been peyntyd on here hedys or abouten here hedys?
PAUPER Þey betokenyn þe blisse þat þey han wytouten ende, for as þat rounde thyng is endeles, so is here blisse endeles, of queche blisse seyȝt Ysaye þe prophete, li [11]: Leticia sempiterna super capita eorum, etc., Endeles merthe shal been on here hedys; þey shullyn had ioye inward and outward wytouten ende: al syhyng and sorwe shal flein away.[19]

DIVES What is the meaning of the round things that are painted on their heads or around their heads?
PAUPER They are a sign of the bliss that they have without end, for as that round thing is endless, so is their bliss endless. Concerning this bliss Isaiah says 'Endless mirth shall be on their heads; they shall have joy inward and outward without end: all sighing and sorrow shall flee away.'

The 'endless bliss' of a permanent state of grace is the endless possession only of those who are free from the possibility of sin, that

is, of those who have ended their earthly lives and have entered
the kingdom of heaven.

With this background in mind we can see in the description of the
pentangle a similar concern with the relationship between the finite,
fragile perfection of the faithful during this life and the endless
perfection of the elect after their judgment. The pentangle is, in
effect, a combination of the two images. Like the halo, it is an
endless figure, and so an appropriate symbol for divine truth and for
the endless perfection of the elect. Like the psaltery, its overall
harmony is a result of the combination of various elements, and so
it is an appropriate symbol for human faith, which is a combination
of virtues and correct practices and which is lost completely (although not irremediably) by a fault or flaw in one of its parts.

3   Endless *Gomen*

All these ideas are linked together in a rather curious use of the word
gomen near the end of the description of the pentangle. The lines
are a bit uncharacteristic of the *Gawain* poet, in that they are repeti-
tious and even a little clumsy; despite the fact that the pentangle's
endlessness has been amply discussed before, the poet returns to
it again, three times in two lines:

> Withouten ende at any noke I oquere fynde,
> Whereuer þe gomen bygan or glod to an ende. (660–1)

> Without end at any angle anywhere, I find, wherever the *gomen* began
> or came to an end.

It is as if he were going out of his way, and even sacrificing poetic
elegance, to call the pentangle an 'endless gomen.'

This use of the word *gomen* is quite unusual; here, and only here,
translators and glossators feel compelled to ignore the word's usual
definitions and to translate it by 'device,' or some such neutral term.
This is to treat the word as if its meaning were totally determined
by its *suppositio* (it does, after all, stand for the pentangle, which
could be called a device), while ignoring its *significatio*. This procedure is not acceptable from the point of view of the logicians, for
a term did not lose its *significatio* when it entered a proposition;
rather, it simply acquired the additional property of *suppositio*. It is
also unacceptable as a piece of modern criticism, for it is extremely
wasteful and misses a fine poetic touch. A fuller examination of

the meanings of the word *gomen* found in the poem shows that here, too, the poet is offering a number of precise ideas about the nature of the relationship between the transcendent and the immanent in human life.

The first relevant definition here is MED 1a, 'Joy, happiness; pleasure, delight, gaiety, mirth.' Many of the citations are references to earthly pleasure, but it is clear also that the word could be used to refer to spiritual joy. From *Titus and Vespasian*, for example, we have 'God in euer þere, beþ þre oþer tweye, That beþ ygadered to speke in his name, In his worshipp for soule game'; 'God is always there, where there are two or three who are gathered in his name, in worship of him, for soul's *game*'; and from *In a morning of May*, 'A woman ... broʒt vs alle to game'; 'A woman ... brought us all to *game*.' The OED, under sense 1 1, also cites *Cursor Mundi*, 'Quen þi meigne was gadird samen / Þam wanted ai þeir gasteli gamen / Til þat iesus was cummen in place'; 'When this company was gathered together, they always lacked their spiritual *gamen* until Jesus had arrived there.' With this sense in mind, 'endless gomen' would be the unending joy of the elect after their judgment, the 'leticia sempi-terna' of Isaiah ascribed by the author of *Dives and Pauper* to the saints. And indeed, in addition to numerous references to 'blisse with-outen ende' we do find in our period a metrical homily that ends

> Forthi red I we al pray
> That he be til us quem that day
> And bring us til his mikel blis,
> That til rihtwis men graithed es.
> Amen say we al samen,
> Thar bes joy and endles gamen.[20]

> Therefore I advise that we all pray that he be gentle to us on that day and bring us to his great bliss which is granted to righteous men. Let us all say amen together; there is joy and endless *gamen*.

The pentangle as a sign for the permanent state of grace of the saved is therefore appropriately called an endless *gomen*, but it must be noted that as a token of other-worldly bliss it contrasts strongly with the situation of its bearer at this point in his life:

> Now ridez þis renk þurʒ þe ryalme of Logres,
> Sir Gauan, on Godez halue, þaʒ hym no gomen þoʒt. (691–2)

Now this knight rides through the kingdom of Logres, Sir Gawain, in God's name, although it seemed no *gomen* to him.

The second meaning for the word is MED 3a, 'An athletic contest; also, a game of chess, backgammon, dice, etc.; a tournament or jousting,' or, more analytically, OED 4, 'A diversion of the nature of a contest, played according to rules, and displaying in the result the superiority either in skill, strength, or good fortune of the winner or winners.' In this case there are sufficient relevant examples from *Sir Gawain and the Green Knight* itself. When the Green Knight first arrives at Arthur's court, he explains that he has no hostile intent, but only wants to play a game: 'Bot if þou be so bold as alle burnez tellen, / Þou wyl grant me godly þe gomen þat I ask / bi ryȝt' (272–4); 'But if you are as bold as all men say, you will graciously grant me the *gomen* that I ask, by right.' He uses the same language a few lines later, saying, 'I craue in þis court a Crystemas gomen' (283); 'I desire in this court a Christmas *gomen*.' After Gawain has argued that the proper person to accept the challenge is himself, the nobles are described as agreeing 'to ryd þe kyng wyth croun, / and gif Gawan þe game' (364–5); 'to relieve the crowned king, and give the *game* to Gawain.' Even after the strange way in which the first half of the bargain proceeds, the agreement is still referred to under the heading of 'Crystmasse gomnez' (683); 'Christmas *gomens*.'

In this sense an 'endless gomen' would be a contest that had no beginning and will have no conclusion, in which there will therefore be no winner and no loser. Here again the implied meaning contrasts sharply with Gawain's actual predicament. His game had a fixed beginning the previous New Year's Day and it will come to an end the next New Year's Day. Despite his shield and its promise he is still bound up, in the world of time, in a *gomen* with fixed limits. And as the poet reminds us, in human *gomens* the end does not often accord with the beginning:

> Gawan watz glad to begynne þose gomnez in halle,
> Bot þaȝ þe ende be heuy haf ȝe no wonder;
> For þaȝ men be mery in mynde quen þay han mayn drynk,
> A ȝere ȝernes ful ȝerne & ȝeldez neuer lyke
> Þe forme to þe fynisment foldez ful selden.   (495–9)

Gawain was glad to begin those *gomens* in the hall, but though the end be heavy, do not wonder at it. For though men are merry in mind when they have strong drink, a year passes quite quickly, and never ends as it began; the beginning seldom resembles the end.

As we listen to the inexorable natural procession of the seasons, it becomes all too clear that Gawain's *gomen*, in this sense, is anything but endless.

The third approach to an explanation of the use of *gomen* in this passage comes from a metaphorical interpretation of several interrelated senses that may be seen as links between the English word *gomen* and the Latin word *bravium*, a word whose theological uses allow for the unification of all the various senses of *gomen*. MED 2c defines *gomen* as 'Any of the sports of hunting, fishing, hawking, or fowling,' a sense that lies behind line 1894 of the poem, '3et is þe lorde on þe launde ledande his gomnes'; 'The lord was still in the field, engaged in his *gomens*'; and line 1319, 'And ay þe lorde of þe londe is lent on his gamnez'; 'And the lord of the land has gone on his *gomens*.' In addition to being the word for the process of hunting, *gomen* is also the term for its goal: MED 6a: '*Coll.* Game animals, birds, or fish, – also, game killed or caught, the kill, the catch.' When Bercilak offers the boar to Gawain, he says, 'Now, Gawayn ... þis gomen is your awen' (1635); 'Now Gawain, this *gomen* is your own.' Process and product were also seen to be linked in the word *bravium*. Its primary meaning is 'prize,' but the *Promptorium Parvulorum* glosses it with 'rennynge, game,' treating it as a combination of 'the fact of striving for a goal' and 'any object of pursuit' (compare MED *gomen* 2c).[21] This same grouping of disparate senses may be found in English passages to be discussed in due course, but the overlap with *bravium* allows a detour into biblical exegesis to find the conceptual framework in which this combination was used to produce spiritual enlightenment, and not just as a piece of linguistic virtuosity.

In First Corinthians there is a passage in which Paul is justifying the vigour and variety of the methods he employs in winning converts to the faith. He ends the section with a comparison between the desire of an athlete to win a race and the desire that a Christian should show for immortal life:

> Nescitis quod ii qui in stadio currunt, omnes quidem currunt, sed unus accipit bravium? Sic currite ut comprehendatis. Omnis autem qui in agone contendit, ab omnibus se abstinet, et illi quidem ut

corruptibilem coronam accipiant: nos autem incorruptam. Ego igitŭr
sic curro, non quasi in incertum. (1 Cor 9:24–6)

Know you not that they that run in the race, all run indeed, but one
receiveth the prize? So run that you may obtain. And every one
that striveth for the mastery, refraineth himself from all things: and
they indeed that they may receive a corruptible crown; but we an
incorruptible one. I therefore so run, not as at an uncertainty.

The stress in this passage in its original context is on the necessity
for self-discipline, given that the promised reward is an incorruptible
crown, and for the outstanding individual to work for the salvation
of others without losing his own through a lack of self-control.

When these words become one of the ordinary readings for Septuagesima Sunday, the analogy with the racecourse could be extended
and the nature of the reward spelled out more clearly. In the sermon
of Radulphus Ardens, for example, we are told that

Stadium est spatium vitae presentis; Bravium est praemium aeternae
beatitudinis. Via, fides; Christus, dux ... Sed tamen non omnes ad
coelestis vitae bravium tendimus ... Omnes igitur qui fidem non ha-
bent ... extra viam sunt. Quod si aliquando aliqua bona opera ex na-
turali pietate faciunt, non plus eis valet quam celerrimus cursus
extra viam: Non enim vadunt, sed errant. Illorum vero qui in via
fidei sunt, alii currunt velociter, alii tarde, alii retrograde. Velociter
currunt, qui abjectis omnibus impedimentis cum toto desiderio ad
coelestia tendunt ... Tarde vero currunt illi, quos cura uxorum,
filiorum, familiarum et mudanorum negotiorum ab appetitu supernae
patriae retardat, nec tamen eos omnino retardat ... Retrograde autem
currunt, qui etsi in via Dei sunt per fidem, tamen ad mundana
desideria redeunt per concupiscentiam. Illi sunt qui affectus uxorum,
liberorum, divitiarum, honorum et voluptatum Deo praeponunt,
nec quae Dei, sed quae mundi sunt, toto desiderio requirunt, et
juxta Apostolum, *Confitentur se nosse Deum, factis autem negant*
(Tit. 1).[22]

The race is the duration of this present life; the prize is the reward of
eternal beatitude. The path is faith; Christ is the leader ... Yet we
are not all aiming at the prize of heavenly life ... For all those who do
not have faith ... are off the path. Since if they sometimes do some

good works from natural piety, it is of no more use to them than
very fast running off the path; for they are not advancing, but wan-
dering. Of those who are on the path of faith, some are running
quickly, some slowly, some backwards. They are running quickly
who have cast aside all impediments and are striving for heaven with
all their desire ... They are running slowly whom concern for wives,
children, families and earthly affairs holds back from the longing
for the celestial home, and yet it does not entirely delay them ... They
are running backwards who, even though they are in the path of
God through faith, still return to earthly desires through concupiscence. They are those who put love of wives, children, riches, honours,
and pleasures ahead of God, who seek the things of the world, not
the things of God, with their whole desire, and, as the apostle says,
'They profess that they know God: but in their works they deny
him.' (Titus 1:16)

The prize, at the fixed limit for this race (that is, at the end of this
present life), is the endless blessedness of the life to come. Some
people will not reach the true goal at all, for they do not have faith
and all of their efforts will be wasted; others will arrive at the proper
point and will receive the reward, though there may be considerable
variation in their speeds because of lapses in the face of various
temptations. But all who reach the goal will receive the reward;[23]
the Gospel reading for this same Sunday is the parable of the vineyard, incidentally one of the *Gawain* poet's favourite texts.

John Mirk, in the Septuagesima sermon in his *Festial*, connects
this passage from Paul with a statement of the necessity of working
in the vineyard, each man after his own degree, and uses *gomen*
to mean both the effort and the reward:

> To þis labour Seynt Paule, yn hys pystyll of þys day, techeþe and
> saythe þus: 'Sic currite, ut comprehendatys.' 'Rennyth soo þat ȝe may
> gripe þe gome.' By þys gomen and rennynge ȝe schull vndyrstond
> bysy labour. For he þat rennyþe for þe gamen, he enforsuþe hym yn
> all his myght to ren swyftly. So most yche good seruand enforse hym
> forto laboure yn þe degree þat God hath sette hym yn.[24]

> Saint Paul, in his epistle for today, teaches about this labour, saying
> 'Run so that you may grasp the *gomen*.' By this *gomen* and running

you shall understand busy labour. For he who runs for the *gomen*
uses all his might to run swiftly. So must each good servant endea-
vour to labour in the degree that God has set him in.

Using *gomen* for both the goal and the process is not a personal
aberration of Mirk's, since both meanings also occur in a sermon on
the same text, ascribed to Wyclif, as part of a general discussion
of biblical signs and their function in the world:

> Þis epistle of Poul telliþ how þat men shulden lyve here, and be God-
> dis laborers for to wynne þe blisse of hevene. Poul bigynneth on
> þis maner, – *Witen ȝe not þat þei þat rennen in þe ferlong for þe pris,
> certis þei rennen all, but oon of hem takiþ þe gleyve? Renne ȝe on
> anoþer maner, þat ȝe all take þe victorie.* It is a knowun þing in
> cuntreis, þat men usen ofte þis gamen, þat two men, holden moost
> swift, rennen a space for a priis, and he þat comeþ first to his
> ende shal have þe gamen þat is sett.[25]

> This epistle of Paul tells how men should live here, and be God's
> labourers to win the bliss of heaven. Paul begins in this way: 'Do you
> know that they who run in a race, for the prize, certainly all run,
> but one of them takes the prize? Run in another way, so that you
> may all win the victory.' It is known in countries that men often fol-
> low this *gomen*, that two men who are considered very swift run a
> distance for a prize, and he who comes first to the end will have the
> *gomen* that is set.

With these various senses in mind, it is possible to summarize the
Gawain poet's organization of all the meanings of *gomen*. Gawain's
life is bound up in a limited *gomen* of precisely one year's duration,
which corresponds to Radulphus's 'spatium vitae praesentis.' The
year between the beginning and the end of this period is poetically
assimilated to a full lifetime, by a manner of thinking closely associated with Septuagesima, since, as John Beleth explains,

> Septuagesima igitur representat tempus deuiationis siue tempus pene
> et culpe ... Septuagesima dicitur, quia septies decem dies habet.
> Hec autem LXX dierum, quam presens agit ecclesia, representat sep-
> tuaginta annos, quibus Israel fuit sub servitute Babylonis ... Sed
> et nostra septuagesima dierum et eorum septuagesima annorum quasi

quedam historia totum generis humani ab Adam usque ad finem
mundi figurat exilium.[26]

Septuagesima therefore represents the time of deviation or the time
of punishment and fault ... It is called Septuagesima since it has seven
tens of days. These seventy days that the church now observes
represent the seventy years in which Israel was in servitude to Baby-
lon ... But both our Septuagesima of days and their Septuagesima
of years as a kind of history are a figure of the whole exile of the
human race from Adam to the end of the world.

The end of Gawain's *gomen*, his meeting with the Green Knight, is
like the end of the allegorical racecourse. It, too, is assimilated to
the end of life and the end of time, by Gawain's expectation of death
and by the poet's sombre language as he ends the pentangle passage:

> Now grayþed is Gawan gay,
> And laȝt his launce ryȝt þore,
> And gef hem alle goud day,
> He wende for euer more.   (665–9)

Now Gawain is made ready, and he took his lance right there; he
bade them all good day, he thought for evermore.

At the end of a struggle of this sort, the *gomen* that is set is a
reward for the successful completion of the course. On the earthly
level the best that Gawain can hope for is survival, continued earthly
life. But the reward symbolized here for winning the race is a new
sort of life, eternal blessedness and *gomen* of a heavenly kind.
Gawain's concern to preserve his earthly life is therefore on a level
quite different from the level of the pentangle's promise of endless
bliss. Conduct during the race must be in accord with the demands
of the final goal, but to value continued earthly life is to enjoy the
running for its own sake and to risk overall failure, to miss the prize
that is set.

Paul's next topic, after the discussion of the racecourse image, was
the ways in which the history of Israel could serve as an example
to the faithful:

Nolo enim vos ignorare fratres, quoniam patres nostri omnes sub

nube fuerunt, et omnes mare transierunt, et omnes in Moyse baptizati
sunt in nube, et in mari: et omnes eamdem escam spiritalem mandu-
caverunt, et omnes eumdem potum spiritalem biberunt (bibebant
autem de spiritali, consequente eos, petra: petra autem erat Christus):
sed non in pluribus eorum beneplacitum est Deo: nam prostrati
sunt in deserto. Haec autem in figura facta sunt nostri, ut non simus
concupiscentes malorum, sicut et illi concipuerunt.   (1 Cor 10:1–6)

For I would not have you ignorant, brethren, that our fathers were all
under the cloud, and all passed through the sea. And all in Moses
were baptized, in the cloud and in the sea: And all did eat the same
spiritual food, And all drank the same spiritual drink; (and they
drank of the spiritual rock that followed them, and the rock was
Christ). But with most of them God was not well pleased: for they
were overthrown in the desert. Now these things were done in a
figure of us, that we should not covet evil things as they also coveted.

The Wycliffite preacher is quick to pick up on this topic, arguing
at length of the figural interpretation of a variety of the events of the
Exodus. His main interest is in those events that are figures of
sacraments, for it is the sacraments, he says, that make a man capable of the effort of striving for the prize:

And so God of blis haþ ordeyned, in tyme of his boþe lawes, how
men shulden have sacramentis to make hem able for þis traveile ...
Bileve techiþ Cristene men þat signes of þe olde lawe weren toknes of
oure signes now, as þei ben tokenes of þe blisse of hevene. Þe
cloude þat ledde hem in desert upon daies, as Goddis law telliþ,
figuride þe water of Cristis side, bi whiche we ben baptisid now. Þe
passing þourȝ þe Reed see and stondinge stable as a walle, figuride
þe passioun of Crist, bi whiche we weren waishen fro synne ... And
þus seiþ Poul here soþely to good entent þat þe stone was Crist, for it
figuride in þis Crist.[27]

And so God of bliss has ordained, in the time of both of his laws,
how men should have sacraments to make them able for this work ...
Belief teaches Christian men that the signs of the old law were
tokens of our signs now, as they are tokens of the bliss of heaven.
The cloud that led them in the desert by day, as God's law tells, was
a figure of the water from Christ's side, by which we are now
baptized. The passing through the Red Sea as it stood like a wall was

a figure of the passion of Christ, by which we were cleansed of sin ... And so Saint Paul says truly here, and with good intent, that the stone was Christ, for in this it was a figure of Christ.

Gawain's 'token of the bliss of heaven,' which makes him fit for the labour he is undertaking, is the pentangle itself, which is a sign for the endless truth in which the elect will ultimately participate. This Shield of Truth is not his possession by nature but is his by grace; this qualification means that it must be called a Shield of Faith. It is by faith that he will stay on the racecourse, if indeed he does stay on it. Further, his faith is comparable to the Truth for which he is aiming. They may both be signified by the same sign, whether the pentangle or the vocal sign 'trawþ,' the differences between the meanings being contingent on the propositions in which the sign is used. In the course of human life, too, the difference between faith and truth is a matter of context. The authoritative statement on this matter comes from St Augustine:

Dixit quidam et illorum qui quondam apud graecos sapientes habiti sunt: *Quantum ad id quod ortum est aeternitas ualet, tantum ad fidem ueritas.* Et profecto est uera sententia. Quod enim nos temporale dicimus, hoc ille *quod ortum est* appelauit. Ex quo genere etiam nos sumus non tantum secundum corpus sed etiam secundum animi mutabilitatem; non enim proprie uocatur aeternum quod aliqua ex parte mutatur. In quantum igitur mutabiles sumus in tantum ab aeternitate distamus. Promittitur autem nobis uita aeterna per ueritatem a cuius perspicuitate rursus tamen distat fides nostra quantum ab aeternitate mortalitas. Nunc ergo adhibemus fidem rebus temporaliter gestis propter nos et per ipsam mundamur et cum ad *speciem* uenerimus quemadmodum succedit fidei ueritas ita mortalitati succedat aeternitas. Quapropter quoniam fides noster fiet ueritas cum ad id quod nobis credentibus promittitur uenerimus, promittitur autem nobis uita aeterna, et dixit ueritas (non quae fiet sicut futura est fides nostra, sed quae semper est ueritas quia ibi est aeternitas) dixit ergo ueritas: *Haec est autem uita aeterna ut cognoscant te unum uerum deum et quem misisti Iesum Christum;* cum fides nostra uidendo fiet ueritas, tunc mortalitatem nostram commutatam tenebit aeternitas.[28]

A certain one of those who were formerly regarded as wise men by the Greeks has said: 'As eternity is to that which has a beginning, so

truth is to faith.' And he has indeed spoken truly, for what we call
temporal, he has described as that which has a beginning. And to this
class we also belong, not only according to the body, but also according to the mutability of the soul. For that is not properly called
eternal which is changed in some part. Insofar, therefore as we are
changeable, insofar is the distance between us and eternity. But
eternal life is promised to us by means of the truth, and once again
our faith is just as far away from the clear knowledge of the truth as
mortality is from eternity. Hence, we now practise faith in the
things that were done in time for our sake, and by it we are cleansed,
in order that when we have come to sight, as the truth follows the
faith, so may eternity follow mortality. Wherefore, our faith will
become truth when we shall arrive at that which is promised us who
believe, but that which is promised to us is eternal life. For the
Truth has said – not that future truth, such as our faith is to become,
but the Truth that is always, because in it is eternity – that Truth,
therefore, has said: 'Now this is eternal life, that they may know thee,
the one true God, and him whom thou hast sent, Jesus Christ.'
When our faith by seeing shall be transformed into truth, then eternity shall hold fast to our own mortality that has then been changed.[29]

In the realm of pure signification the pentangle is a sign for Truth,
absolute *veritas*, imposed according to right reason since its percep-
tible qualities are analogous to the imperceptible qualities of Truth.
Its meaning, however, is more than this, for it is also a communicative sign with a salutary effect on anyone who looks at it with
understanding. Like any other proper religious image, it has the
power to evoke thought of God in those who respond to it positively.
It is therefore not only a sign for Truth *per se* but also for Truth as
the object of religious faith and as the support for those who wish to
maintain their faith.

Just as it is possible to speak, by extension, of the 'truth of this
thing or of that thing,' so it is possible to use the pentangle also as a
sign for a quality belonging to an individual man. When it is used
in a proposition as an attribute of a living human, it must stand
for faith, the virtue by which humans are most closely connected to
and imitative of their creator. The pentangle, like the word *trawþ*,
is therefore ambiguous, though it is far from vague. When it is
attributed to God, it means Truth, and when it is attributed to a
man, it means faith. As long as we are alive and subject to the world

of mutability, we live in faith; once we have arrived at the promised goal of eternal life, we shall live in Truth. The pentangle is best seen as a sacramental badge, a visible indication of the inward spiritual grace granted to Gawain before his departure on the quest. It is also, because of its ambiguous meaning, an excellent focus for meditation on the relationship between the limited and fragile faith that may be our possession temporarily in this life and the endless Truth in which we may participate in the life to come.

4   The Girdle and the Wound

The analysis of the meaning of the pentangle, both in isolation and in context, can proceed fairly straightforwardly in line with the various techniques of the fourteenth-century logicians, but when we turn to the explanation of the green girdle, a number of difficulties arise. On first glance it would seem that the relationship of sign to referent should be easier to determine because we are allowed to witness its imposition as a sign, whereas in the case of the pentangle we learn about it at second hand. Nevertheless, despite the great amount of detail we are given about the girdle and the various statements made about its meaning, it is much more difficult to find a unified perspective on all the relevant data. Even at it most basic level, the meaning of the girdle as a sign remains problematic.[1]

We first hear about Lady Bercilak's green girdle not as a *signum* but simply as a *res* when Gawain refuses to accept her (more valuable) ring. In its place she offers him her girdle:

> 'If ȝe renay my rynk, to riche for hit semez,
> Ȝe wolde not so hyȝly halden be to me,
> I schal gif yow my girdel, þat gaynes yow lasse.'
> Ho laȝt a lace lyȝtly þat leke vmbe hir sydez,
> Knit vpon hir kyrtel vnder þe clere mantyle,
> Gered hit watz with grene sylke and with golde schaped,
> Noȝt bot arounde brayden, beten with fyngrez;
> And þat ho bede to þe burne, and blyþely bisoȝt
> Þaȝ hit vnworþi were, þat he hit take wolde.   (1827–35)

> If you refuse my ring, because it seems too valuable and you do not want to be so obligated to me, I will give you my girdle, which

profits you less.' She lightly took hold of a sash that was fastened around her waist and tied around her gown under her bright mantle. It was made of green silk and of gold, decorated only at the edges and embroidered by hand; and she offered it to the man and blithely implored him to take it, though it was unworthy.

Gawain refuses to take the gift, categorizing it only as a valuable object and paying no attention to its particular qualities. This prompts the lady to describe it more fully, turning from the object itself to its invisible powers:

'Now forsake ȝe þis silke,' sayde þe burne þenne,
'For hit is symple in hitself? And so hit wel semez.
Lo! so hit is littel, and lasse hit is worþy;
Bot who-so knew þe costes þat knit ar þerinne,
He wolde hit prayse at more prys, parauenture;
For quat gome so is gorde with þis grene lace,
While he hit hade hemely halched aboute,
Þer is no haþel vnder heuen tohewe hym þat myȝt,
For he myȝt not be slayn for slyȝt vpon erþe.'   (1846–54)

'Do you now refuse this silk,' said the lady then, 'because it is simple in itself? And so it certainly is. See, it is little, and even less in value. But if a man knew the properties that are knit into it, he would perhaps value it more highly. For whatever man is girt with this green lace, while he keeps it closely fastened about himself, there is no man under heaven who could cut him down, for he could not be slain by any stratagem on earth.'

This elaboration, and the connection of the girdle's powers with the particular danger in which Gawain finds himself, open up the possibility that it is to be seen as an appropriate sign for a man's desire for continued earthly life, but there are no explicit directions to see it as anything other than a very special *res*. The visible and tangible qualities of the object are clearly of no interest to Gawain either here or later, for the poet informs us that his reason for wearing it is simply to save his life:

Þe gordel of þe grene silke, þat gay wel bisemed,
Vpon þat ryol red cloþe þat ryche watz to schewe.
Bot wered not þis ilk wyȝe for wele þis gordel,

For pryde of þe pendauntez, þaȝ polyst þay were,
And þaȝ þe glyterande golde glent vpon endez,
Bot for to sauen hymself, when suffer hym byhoued,
To byde bale withoute dabate of bronde hym to were
    oþer knyffe. (2035–42)

The girdle of green silk suited that gallant man well, over the royal red cloth that was splendid to see. But this man did not wear the girdle for its value, for pride in its pendants, though they were polished, though the glittering gold shone at the edges, but to save himself when he had to suffer and endure death, without resisting or defending himself with sword or knife.

We next hear about the green girdle after the test of the Green Chapel, when Gawain has survived his ordeal with only a slight cut to his neck. That he is cut at all is said to be due to his possession of the girdle, which ought by rights have been returned to Bercilak:

At þe þrid þou fayled þore,
And þerfor þat tappe ta þe.
For hit is my wede þat þou werez, þat ilke wouen girdel,
Myn owen wyf hit þe weued, I wot wel for soþe. (2356–9)

But on the third, you failed then, and therefore you took that blow. For it is my clothing that you wear, that very woven girdle: my own wife wove it for you, I know well and truly.

At this point Gawain moves a step closer to turning the girdle into a sign. He unties it and hurls it away as he laments his own cowardice and covetousness: if we see this action as a visible representation of his speech, then he is equating the girdle with cowardice and casting them both away:

'Corsed worth cowarddyse and couetyse boþe!
In yow is vylany and vyse þat vertue disstryez.'
Þenne he kaȝt to þe knot and þe kest lawsez,
Brayde broþely þe belt to þe burne seluen. (2374–7)

'Cursed be cowardice and covetousness both! In you is villainy and vice that destroys virtue.' Then he caught hold of the knot and undid the clasp and angrily threw the belt to the man himself.

This meaning is never explicitly imposed, however, since as soon as the girdle is in the Green Knight's possession, he attempts to give it a different meaning and to return it to the repentant Gawain. In this case it is the evocative power of the sign that is at issue; Gawain is to treat it as a memento of the entire encounter:

> And I gif þe, sir, þe gurdel þat is golde-hemmed,
> For hit is grene as my goune. Sir Gawayn, ȝe maye
> Þenk vpon þis ilke þrepe, þer þou forth þryngez
> Among prynces of prys, and þis a pure token
> Of þe chaunce of þe grene chapel at cheualrous knyȝtez.
> (2395–9)

> And, sir, I give you the gold-hemmed girdle, for it is green as my gown. Sir Gawain, think upon this contest when you ride among worthy princes, and this will be a perfect sign to chivalrous knights of the adventure at the green chapel.

This imposition fails, I believe, because it does not take into account all of the necessary prerequisites for a rational decision about signs and meanings. The tie between the sign and the supposed referent is only that the former is green and the latter (that is, the 'chaunce') is loosely related to some other green objects (that is, the 'goune' and the 'chapel'). Whatever else the entire test may have signified, greenness is certainly not as essential a characteristic to it as the endlessness of *trawþ* is to the pentangle, or even as the *humus* out of which *homo* was first created. It would seem that there is an absence of 'right reason' here, for this attempt to make the girdle a sign does not even succeed with Gawain, who is its first intended audience: the girdle cannot be a simple memento for the affair at the Green Chapel, because it is not accepted as a stable sign with such a meaning.

After his stanza of complaint against Lady Bercilak and his self-excuse in accordance with biblical parallels, Gawain accepts the girdle but explicitly rejects Bercilak's attempt to provide it with a meaning. Not that he wants the girdle as a *res*: he still argues that he is not interested in it for its appearance or its value:

'Bot your gordel,' quoþ Gawayn, 'God yow forȝelde!
Þat wyl I welde wyth guod wylle, not for þe wynne golde,
Ne þe saynt, ne þe sylk, ne þe syde pendaundes,
For wele ne for worchyp, ne for wlonk werkkez.'   (2429–32)

'But as for your girdle,' said Gawain, 'God reward you! I will wear it
in good will, not for the fine gold, or the material, the silk, nor
the pendants, nor for its cost or worth or good workmanship.'

Rather he will accept it as a sign, and attributes to it a new meaning,
saying that he will make use of it for its ability to remind him to
be humble:

Bot in syngne of my surfet I schal se hit ofte,
When I ride in renoun, remorde to myseluen
Þe faut and þe fayntyse of þe flesche crabbed,
How tender hit is to entyse teches of fylþe;
And þus, quen pryde schal me pryk for prowes of armes,
Þe loke to þis luf-lace schal leþe my hert.   (2433–8)

But as a sign of my fault I will look at it often, when I ride in
renown, to remember with remorse the fault and the frailty of perverse flesh, how liable it is to catch the spots of filth; and so, when
pride in my prowess of arms shall stir me, the sight of this love-lace
will humble my heart.

This imposition looks rather more promising, and I think that most
readers of the poem view this as the last word on the girdle's meaning: it is a visible representation of the particular sin that Gawain
has committed, appropriate to the referent because it is the object
wrongfully taken, which he will keep in order to remind himself
of the frailty of the flesh and the ease with which it is corrupted.
This is the meaning the girdle still has as Gawain rides toward
Camelot:

Þe hurt watz hole þat he hade hent in his nek,
And þe blykkande belt he bare þeraboute,
Abelef as a bauderyk bounden by his syde,
Loken vnder his lyfte arme, þe lace, with a knot,
In tokenyng he watz tane in tech of a faute.   (2484–8)

The wound that he had received in the neck was healed, and he wore
the shining belt around it, crosswise like a baldric and fastened
under his left arm, the lace, with a knot, in tokening that he had
been found guilty of a fault.

Nevertheless, the description of the meaning of the girdle has
changed significantly when Gawain comes to explain it to Arthur
and his court. He is no longer concerned with its ability to remind
him of the adventure or to combat his pride, but only with its
semantic value. Further, he does not even use it as a sign for the
frailty of the flesh or for his particular sinful act. Rather, he now
declares that it is a sign of permanent *untrawþ* – in effect, the inverse
of the pentangle as a sign of endless *trawþ*:

> 'Lo! lorde,' quoþ þe leude, and þe lace hondeled,
> 'Þis is þe bende of þis blame I bere in my nek,
> Þis is þe laþe and þe losse þat I laȝt haue
> Of couardise and couetyse þat I haf caȝt þare;
> Þis is þe token of vntrawþe þat I am tan inne,
> And I mot nedez hit were wyle I may last;
> For mon may hyden his harme, bot vnhap ne may hit,
> For þer hit onez is tachched twynne wil hit neuer.'   (2505–12)

> 'My lord,' said the man, and handled the lace, 'this that I wear on my
> neck is the mark of my fault, this is the injury and the loss I have
> taken because of the cowardice and covetousness that I caught there.
> This is the token of *untrawþ* that I have been taken in, and I must
> needs wear it as long as I live. For a man may hide his harm, but
> may not unfasten it, for where it is once fixed, it will never leave.'

This is the final attempt at making the girdle a sign, and it is the
most obvious failure of all. It does not cause its audience to think of
the *untrawþ* for which it is supposed to stand, since they go so far as
to reverse the meaning, and the green baldric becomes a sign
of honour for the lords and ladies of Arthur's court:

> Þe kyng comfortez þe knyȝt, and alle þe court als
> Laȝen loude þerat, and luflyly acorden
> Þat lordes and ladis þat longed to þe Table,
> Vche burne of þe broþerhede, a bauderyk schulde haue,

A bende abelef hym aboute of a bryȝt grene,
And þat, for sake of þat segge, in swete to were.
For þat watz acorded þe renoun of þe Rounde Table,
And he honoured þat hit hade euermore after.   (2513–20)

The king comforts the knight, and all the court also laugh loudly at
it, and amiably agree that the lords and the ladies who belonged
to the Round Table, every man of the brotherhood, should have a
baldric, and wear a band, crosswise about him, for the sake of that
man. For that was considered to be renown for the Round Table,
and the man that had it was honoured for ever.

The court's rejection of this meaning for the girdle and their inability
to learn a serious lesson from Gawain's experience arise from their
own spiritual condition, but the fact that they are able to reject it as
a sign is an indication that Gawain has failed in his task as first
institutor. This failure can be explained in terms of the very dichot-
omy that emerged from the discussion of the meaning of the pentangle, that between the permanence of the supernatural and the
transitoriness of the human.

When we look through the literature of our poet's period, we find
that there is indeed such a thing as permanent untrawþ and that
there are creatures of whom it might be said that the sin that is
attached to them will never be separated. Such creatures might
appropriately wear visible indications of sinfulness forever. The difficulty here is, in a manner parallel to the difficulty with the idea of
endless trawþ, that Gawain does not belong to either of the appropriate categories. Just as the fact that he is not God prevents him
from being considered endlessly true, so the fact that he is not Satan
prevents him from being endlessly untrue, for as Dives and Pauper
makes clear, it is Satan who is sovereign untrawþ:

DIUES Syth þe fend knowith so many trewþis and whot what is don,
for he is at euery wikkyd dede, me meruelyth mychil why he is so
redy to lye and why he is so fals.
PAUPER For he hatiþ God þat is souereyn trewþe. And for þat he
myȝth nouȝt be efne with God in souereynte of trewþe ne han þe
name of souereyn trewþe þat is God, þerfor his lykyng and his
trauayle is to ben souereyn falshed and souereynly fals. And þerfor
Crist seyth in þe gospel þat þe fend stood neuer in trewþe, for þer is
no trewþe in hym.

DIVES   Since the fiend knows so many truths, and knows what is
done, since he is present at every wicked deed, I wonder greatly why
he is so ready to lie and why he is so false.
PAUPER   Because he hates God, who is sovereign truth. Because he
might not be equal with God in sovereignty of truth or have the
name of sovereign truth that is God, therefore he desires and works
to be sovereign falsehood and sovereignly false. And therefore Christ
says in the gospel that the fiend never stood in truth, for there is
no truth in him.

Similarly, just as it is only after death that the elect begin to share
in the 'endless gamen' that is their union with God, so too it is only
after death that the damned lose all hope of salvation and are faced
with

> ouyrdon hete of fer & gronchyng of teth for [c]old & for peyne,
> þerknesse & smoke & byttyr wepynge withoutyn ende, rorynge &
> belwynge of foule fendys & wepynge and weylynge, sobbynge and
> syȝhynge of synful soulys & endles reprof of her synnys, endeles
> dryhed, endles threst, stync, leuen, þondyr, & worm of conscience,
> boundys, prysoun, dred, schame, wantynge of þe blysful syȝthe
> of Godys face & wo withoutyn hope of any wel.[2]

> excessive heat and fire and gnashing of teeth for cold and pain,
> darkness and smoke and bitter weeping without end, roaring and
> bellowing of foul fiends and sighing of sinful souls and endless
> reproof of their sins, endless dryness, endless thirst, stink, lightning,
> thunder, and worm of conscience, bonds, prison, dread, shame,
> lack of the blissful sight of God's face, and woe without hope of good.

While a man is alive, therefore, he must make use of the time that
he has, for he may not amend himself afterwards, as a contemporary
sermon warns:

> Arise þan, for now is tyme of mercy, whils þat þou lyvest here; for
> more [ty]me þan we gett whils þat we liff here shall we neuer haue
> aftur þat we are passed hens, but oure owne werkes shall folowe
> vs where-euer þat we goye.[3]

> Arise, then, for now is the time of mercy, while you live here; for we

shall never get more time than we have here, once we have passed away, but our own works will follow us wherever we go.

As long as we are alive, of course, we are always able to repent and find salvation, as we are reminded frequently in the sermons of the day and in authoritative doctrinal statements throughout the history of Christian thought:

> Nullus ergo peccator desperet, quando fornicata cum multis amatoribus recipitur, quia fons pietatis misericordiae Jesus Cristus nullius iniquitatibus exhauritur, nullius sceleribus polluitur, sed semper purus, et abundans gratia dulcedinis, omnes ad se revertentes infirmos et peccatores recipit, et quibuscunque peccatis sint maculati, abluit. Et ut certi sint omnes peccatores et iniqui se veniam peccatorum suorum accipere, si ipsa peccata sua curant dimittere, et poenitentiam agere, ipse fons pietatis, pro amore quem erga eos habebat, eamdem carnem quam pro eis sumpsit, sicut superius exposui, pertulit crucifigi, ut qui erant peccatis mortui, nec aliter ad vitam redire poterant, nisi pretio sanguinis eius redempti, nullo modo desperent, cernentes pretium quod est datum pro peccatis suis.[4]

> Therefore let no sinner despair, when the one who fornicated with many lovers is received, since Jesus Christ the fountain of pity and mercy is not exhausted by anyone's iniquities, is not polluted by anyone's crimes, but, always pure and abounding in the grace of sweetness, receives all the sick and sinful who are stained with sin. And so that all sinners and evil men may be sure that they will receive pardon for their sins if they take care to abandon their sins and to do penance, the fountain of pity, for the love that he had for them, allowed that flesh to be crucified which he had assumed on their behalf, as I explained before, so that those who were dead in sin and might not otherwise come back to life except through being bought at the cost of his life should not despair, recognizing the price that has been paid for their sins.

This attitude finds its way into more popular works, such as narrative sermons, in the form of exemplary stories that demonstrate that, no matter how grievous the sin, repentance and confession may blot it out. In *Jacob's Well* we are told of a woman who slept with her own son and had a child by him, which she killed to hide her guilt.

When she was denounced by a fiend to the emperor, the fact that she had repented, confessed, and done penance made it impossible for her accuser even to recognize her at court, and 'Þe womman hadde an hyȝ worschype, & was sauyd fro temperall deth & fro endles deth, & made clene, wyth þe scope of penaunce, of her cursyd synne'; 'The woman was greatly honoured, and was saved from earthly death and from endless death, and made clean of her cursed sin by the scoop of penance.'[5]

    Stories of biblical sinners who repented their earlier sins are often found in the sermon literature of the period, one of the most frequent examples being Mary Magdalene. She is the focus, for example, of the homily for Advent quoted above in connection with the phrase 'endless gamen.' The preacher sums up her story as follows:

> Hir rewed of hir self ful sare,
> And hauid for hir sin slik kare
> That nan that hers spek of Marie,
> Thar haf wanhop of Godes mercie,
> For do man neuer sa mikel sin,
> And he wil his sin blin,
> Godd of heuin es ai redi
> For to haf on him mercie,
> That was sen in the Maudelayn,
> That bird mak sinful man ful fain.[6]

> She repented full sorrowfully, and was so worried about her sin that no man who hears about Mary shall be in despair of God's mercy. For no matter how great a sin a man does, if he will repent of his sin, God in heaven is always ready to have mercy on him; that was seen in Magdalen, which ought to give hope to sinful man.

The extreme danger of *wanhope*, that is, the refusal to believe in the possibility of repentance and forgiveness, is most vividly portrayed through the conventional explanation of the sins of Judas, deriving ultimately from Jerome but repeated frequently in our period. *Jacob's Well* warns against falling into *wanhope*, saying that it

> makyth a man noȝt to trusten in goddys mercy; for hym thynketh his sinne is so myche, þat he may neuere haue forȝevenesse, & so, perauenture, he may sle hym-self thruȝ þe feendys combryng.

makes a man not trust in God's mercy; for it seems to him that
his sin is so great that he may never have forgiveness, and so, perhaps,
he may slay himself through the snares of the fiend.

Such a man refuses to believe that he will ever be forgiven, for it
seems that this could happen only if God were not just. But

> Seynt Jerom seyth, super Ps. lxx., þat Judas trespacyd more whan he
> hynge hym-self, þanne whanne he betrayed crist, & dyspeyr was
> cause þat he slewe him-self. Þerfor wanhope þat duryth in þe ende, &
> is noȝt amendyd wyth repentaunce, schal neuere be forȝevyn in þis
> world, ne in þe oþer world, Mat. 12. *secundum* doctoures; but þat it
> schal be ponysched.[7]

> Saint Jerome says, commenting on Psalm 70, that Judas trespassed
> more when he hanged himself than when he betrayed Christ, and
> despair was the reason that he slew himself. Therefore, *wanhope* that
> persists until the end and is not amended with repentance will
> never be forgiven in this world, nor in the other world (Matt 12, as
> explained by authorities), but it will be punished.

From the point of view of these commentators, Gawain's belief that
his 'harme' will never be taken from him, a belief that tends towards the sin of *wanhope*, is dangerously false; any attempt to use a
sign for such an impossible meaning must necesarily fail.

   Gawain's insistence, at the end of his journey, that he is still in a
sinful state and that he will always remain so seems even more
surprising, given this context, when we recognize that he has already
been through a form of confession with Bercilak. Even though
Bercilak is not a priest, a fact that might invalidate a real-life confession, Gawain's words and actions after the wounding are analogous
to those of a proper confessional scene. There is a strong impression
that the confession is at least poetically valid, as can be seen from
an analysis of Gawain's response to being caught in his sin. The
necessary elements of confession are described by Peter Lombard and
echoed in many other discussions of the topic, as, for example, in
The Parson's Tale:

> In perfectione autem poenitentiae tria observanda sunt, scilicet
> compunctio cordis, confessio oris, satisfactio operis.[8]

Now shaltow understande what is bihovely and necessarie to verray parfit Penitence. And þis stant on three thynges: / Contricioun of herte, Confessioun of mouth, and Satisfaccioun.⁹

Although the question of a man's contrition of heart may not be decided by another man, it seems that the poet would have us consider Gawain to be contrite, for he tells us that Gawain was overwhelmed by grief and shame:

> So agreued for greme he gryed withinne;
> Alle þe blode of his brest blende in his face,
> Þat al he schrank for schome þat þe schalk talked. (2370–2)

So overcome with grief that he shuddered inwardly, all the blood of his breast rushed to his face so that he shrank for shame at what the man said.

It would seem also that he makes confession of mouth, for when he begins to speak, he condemns his own flaws:

> Þe forme worde vpon folde þat þe freke meled:
> 'Corsed worth cowarddyse and couetyse boþe!
> In yow is vylany and vyse þat vertue disstryez.' (2373–5)

The first word of all that the man said was 'Cursed be cowardice and covetousness both! In you is villainy and vice that destroy virtue.'

Finally, Gawain gives satisfaction through restitution, in that he returns the girdle to Bercilak:

> Þenne he kaȝt to þe knot, and þe kest lawsez,
> Brayde broþely þe belt to þe burne seluen. (2376–7)

Then he grabbed the knot, and undid the clasp, and threw the belt angrily at the man himself.

Both Gawain and Bercilak use the vocabulary of the confessional in this scene: Gawain says, 'I byknowe yow, knyȝt' (2385), and Bercilak says, 'Þou art confessed' (2391) and 'hatz þe penaunce' (2392). The end result of the discussion is that Bercilak can grant Gawain a kind

of absolution and say that he has atoned for his sin and is as pure as
if he had never sinned at all:

> I halde þe polysed of þat plyȝt, and pured as clene
> As þou hadez neuer forfeted syþen þou watz fyrst borne.   (2393–4)

> I consider you cleansed of that offence and purified as clean as if you
> had never sinned since you were first born.

Gawain's attempt to use the green girdle as a sign of his own
inescapable *untrawþ* is an error both on the general grounds that
untrawþ belongs permanently only to Satan and the damned and on
the specific grounds that we have seen him go through a complete
and convincing confession. Gawain's state, once he has arrived back
at the court after falling back into sin, is indeed analogous to the
untrawþ of Satan and the damned, but only in the way that his initial
faith was analogous to the Truth signified by the pentangle: since
he is alive, his condition is temporary and mutable, whether he
recognizes it or not. The poet does not leave his audience in the
negative position of being able to recognize Gawain's error but
unable to determine the true situation. Rather, he includes another,
traditional sign, which can convey to us the correct relationship
between sin and forgiveness, and that is the wound that Gawain has
received in his neck. The use of wounds as metaphors for sin and
the idea that Christ is the healer are widespread in medieval religious
writings.[10] It is a favourite topic for Augustine:

> Sicut autem curatio uia est ad sanitatem, sic ista curatio peccatores
> sanandos reficiendosque suscepit. Et quemadmodum medici cum
> alligant uulnera, non incomposite, sed apte id faciunt, ut uinculi
> utilitatem quaedam pulchritudo etiam consequatur, sic medicina
> sapientiae per hominis susceptionem nostris est accomodata uulneri-
> bus de quibusdam contrariis curans et de quibusdam similibus.
> Sicut etiam ille, qui medetur uulneri corporis, adhibet quaedam con-
> traria sicut frigidum calido, uel humido siccum uel si quid aliud
> huiusmodi, adhibet etiam quaedam similia sicut linteolum uel ro-
> tundo uulneri rotundum, uel oblongum oblongo ligaturamque ipsam
> non eandem membris omnibus, sed similem similibus coaptat, sic
> sapientia dei hominem curans, se ipsam exhibuit ad sanandum, ipsa
> medicus, ipsa medicina.[11]

Just as a cure is a way to health, so also this Cure received sinners to
heal and strengthen them. And just as physicians when they bind
up wounds do not do so haphazardly but neatly so that a certain beauty
accompanies the utility of the bandages, so the medicine of Wisdom
by taking on humanity is accommodated to our wounds, healing some
by contraries and some by similar things. He who tends the wounds
of the body sometimes applies contraries, such as cold to hot, moist to
dry, and so on; at other times he applies similar things, like a round
bandage for a round wound or an oblong bandage for an oblong wound,
not using the same bandage for all members but fitting similar things
to similar. Thus the Wisdom of God, setting out to cure men, applied
Himself to cure them, being at once the Physician and the Medicine.[12]

Sin is also treated as a wound in an allegorization of a secular narrative in a contemporary sermon. We are told that Alexander had a
son called Sares, who, because of his extreme beauty, was called
a son of Jove. But when he was injured in battle, he declared that the
wound proved that he was not divine. The preacher explains:

By þis Sares I vndurstond euery man and woman her on vrthe, þe
wich þat sheweþ gret vtward deuocion and clennes, and invard in
herte þei be full of malis and envye. Qwo ben þise? Trewly þise
fals ypocrites and bacbytors. Þei will come to þe chur[c]he and knokke
hem-selfe vn þe breste and turne þe eyen owteward as þei wold goy
to heven all hote, but ȝitt þe will bacbite here euen-cristen and make
wrouth and debate where-as loue was a-fore. ȝitt þisse maner of
pepull ben holden Goddes children now-a-dais. But trewly and þei
wold be-holde here own soule, þei myght answere þe pepull as Sares
dud, 'Hoc vulnus – id est peccatum – manifestat quod ego non
sum filius Dei nec de progenie illius – my wounde þat þe synne of
my soule is bounden in sheweþ' *et cetera*.[13]

By this Sares I understand every man and woman here on earth who
shows outward devotion and purity, but inward, in the heart, they
are full of malice and envy. Who are these people? Truly, they
are false hypocrites and backbiters. They will come into the church
and beat their breasts and turn their eyes outward as if they wanted
to go to heaven immediately but still they will backbite their fellow
Christians and cause wrath and discord where love was before.
Yet such people are considered God's children these days. But truly,
if they would look at their own souls, they might answer the people

as Sares did: 'My wound, in which the sin of my soul is bound, shows that I am not the son of God nor one of his offspring.'

This same metaphor is used and extended in discussions of proper penitential practice. The decree 'Omnis utriusque sexus' of the Fourth Lateran Council, which gave the impetus to much penitential material in the sermons now available to us, looks at the metaphor of the wound from the perspective of the appropriate behaviour for the priest:

> Sacerdos autem sit discretus et cautus, ut more periti medici super- infundat vinum et oleum vulneribus sauciati, diligenter inquirens et peccatoris circumstantias et peccati, per quas prudenter intelligat, quale illi consilium debeat exhibere et cuiusmodi remedium adhibere, diversis experimentis utendo ad sanandum aegrotum.[14]

> Let the priest be discreet and careful, so that in the manner of a skilled doctor he may pour wine and oil on the wounds of the wounded man, diligently inquiring about the circumstances of both the sinner and the sin, through which he may understand what type of advice he must offer him and what type of remedy he must apply, using a variety of methods to heal the sick man.

The author of *Jacob's Well* speaks in similar terms, but more from the point of view of the sinner:

> for, þowȝ deed flesche be kut out of a wounde, wyth a scharp corryzie, þi wounde, þowȝ, nedyth to be pourgyd, wyth a drawyng salue; ellys it wolde rotyn & festryn aȝen. Ryȝt so, þowȝ þi dedly synne be kut out, with sorwe of herte, fro þe pyt of þi conscyens, ȝit þi conscyens nedyth to be pourgyd, with a drawyng salue of clene schryfte, & elles þe wounde of dedly synne rotyth and festryth aȝen in þi soule.[15]

> for, though the dead flesh be cut out of a wound with a sharp knife, still the wound needs to be purged with a drawing salve, or else it will rot and fester again. Similarly, though your deadly sin be cut, with sorrow of heart, out of the pit of your conscience, still your conscience needs to be purged with the drawing salve of pure shrift, or else the wound of deadly sin rots and festers again in your soul.

Given these various possibilities for extending and expanding
the metaphorical equation of sin and wound, it is interesting to see
the way in which the *Gawain* poet treats Gawain's wound to discover its use as a statement about his sin and the poet's view of sin
in general. It is first introduced into the narrative purely as a *res*,
that is, as a physical wound with no direct suggestion of a metaphor.
The third time that the Green Knight brings his axe down on Gawain's neck, he draws blood:

> He lyftes lyȝtly his lome, and let hit doun fayre
> With þe barbe of þe bitte bi þe bare nek;
> Paȝ he homered heterly, hurt hym no more
> Bot snyrt hym on þat on syde, þat seuered þe hyde.
> Þe scharp schrank to þe flesche þurȝ þe schyre grece,
> Þat þe schene blod ouer his schulderes schot to þe erþe.   (2309–13)

He lifted his weapon lightly, and let it fall down, with the edge of the
blade on the bare neck. Though he hit him heavily, he did not hurt
him, but nicked him on the side so that it cut the skin. The sharp
blade sank into the flesh through the fair fat, so that the bright blood
spurted over his shoulders to the ground.

Shortly thereafter, the Green Knight explains the cause of the wound,
which goes a long way towards explaining its meaning. The first
two strokes of the axe were simple feints: Gawain was not wounded
because he kept to the terms of the agreement with Bercilak to
exchange winnings on the first two occasions:

> Fyrst I mansed þe muryly with a mynt one,
> And roue þe wyth no rof-sore, with ryȝt I þe profered
> For þe forwarde þat we fest in þe fyrst nyȝt,
> and þou trystyly þe trawþe and trwly me haldez,
> Al þe gayne þow me gef, as god mon schulde.
> Þat oþer munt for þe morne, mon, I þe profered,
> Þou kyssedes my clere wyf – þe cossez me raȝtez.
> For boþe two here I þe bede bot two bare myntes
>   boute scaþe   (2345–53)

First I threatened you playfully with a single feint, and did not rip
you open with a harsh wound; I did this rightly because of the

agreement we made on the first night, for you kept to it truly and faithfully, and gave me all the gain, as a good man should. I gave you the second feint, sir, for the next day, when you kissed my fair wife, for you passed the kisses on. For these two I gave you two mere feints, without any harm.

Each day of 'true' behaviour earns him escape from wounding, but since his 'truth' failed on the third day, with the third blow he is wounded:

> Trwe mon trwe restore,
> Þenne þar mon drede no waþe.
> At þe þrid þou fayled þore,
> And þerfor þat tappe ta þe   (2354–7)

A true man must restore truth, and then fear no danger, but on the third, then you failed, and therefore you took that tap.

This causal connection between the wound and the acceptance of the girdle connects Gawain's story more closely with the story of Sares. Sares' wound demonstrated that, although he was reputed to be divine, he was in fact mortal. Gawain's willingness to keep the girdle in violation of his covenant with Bercilak is an indication of his mortality and his all-too-human desire to preserve his mortal life; the cause of his wounding is therefore the same object that demonstrates that he lacks the endless *trawþ*, which, as we have seen, is an attribute of the divine rather than of the human.

The wound and the girdle are connected in yet another way in the last scene of the poem, when Gawain is trying to explain the situation to Arthur. He describes the girdle as 'þe bende of þis blame I bere in my nek' (2506). This is a difficult line; the poem's editors would have us choose between two equally possible interpretations. Gollancz glosses the line as ' "this is the *bende* (i.e. heraldic sign) of this blame-worthiness" (of which he has just spoken).'[16] Wright would have us read, in a version that Moorman considers 'less tortured,' 'This is the ribbon belonging to (or, cause of) this hurt I received in my neck.'[17] It is neither necessary nor productive, however, to choose between these interpretations, since the verbal ambiguities in the phrase relate so well to the complexities of the situation. The 'blame' of which Gawain speaks is both the particular sinful act he performed and the wound in his neck; within the narrative the former caused the latter, and within the literary framework the latter is a metaphor for the former. The lace is not only 'of' this blameworthiness but is also 'of' the wound, since it is an intermediary between the two. The 'bende' is a ribbon, to be sure, but inasmuch as the word is also a heraldic term and since the girdle is explicitly described as being tied in heraldic fashion (2486–7), it would be wasteful to dismiss the heraldic significance of the vocabulary here. Gawain is treating the girdle as a badge denoting both the wound and the sin.

Gawain's need to have a badge as a sign for his sin, and his inability to use the wound itself, reveal much about the poet's view of sin. A wound cannot be an appropriate sign for the kind of permanent sinfulness that Gawain attributes to himself, simply because wounds heal. This is not a fact imposed on the poet's work from the outside world but rather something he mentions explicitly at the very point where the heraldic nature of the wearing of the girdle is first affirmed:

> Þe hurt watz hole þat he hade hent in his nek,
> And þe blykkande belt he bare þeraboute
> Abelef as a bauderyk   (2484–6)

> The hurt that he had received in his neck was healed, and he wore the shining belt crosswise like a baldric.

The green girdle is something that Gawain can choose to wear permanently, so Gawain believes that he can assign 'permanent untrawþ' as its meaning; the wound is already healed and is no longer capable of bearing such a meaning.

To discover what this situation reveals about the poet's concerns with Gawain's predicament, we need only examine the literature in his tradition to determine the conventional meaning of a healed wound. One use of the metaphor may be found in the ubiquitous *Pricke of Conscience*. The author imagines at one point that he has been asked whether the souls in heaven will have any memory of the sins they once committed, and answers, with a reference to Anselm as an appropriate authority, that they must remember the sins of which they have been shriven if they are to feel properly grateful to God for the mercy he has shown them:

> Bot now may þou ask me and lere
> A questyon, and say on þis manere:
> 'Salle þai oght think þat salle be safe,

On þe syns of·whilk þai þam schrafe
Here in þair lyfe, and made þam clene,
And of þam assoyled has bene?'
Saint Anselme answers to þis,
And says þat þou þat have heven blys,
Sale love God and thank him þare
Of alle gudes, both les and mare,
Þat he has done tylle þe here,
And tylle alle other, on þe same manere,
Þe whilk, at þe day of dome, salle be safe,
And with þe endles blys salle have.
Gret gud he dose þe, while þou lyfes,
When he þi syns þe here forgyves;
How moght þou þan, with hert fre,
Thank God of þat þat he has forgyven þe,
Alle þe syns þat þou has wroght,
If þou moght thynk on nane in thoght?

But now you may ask me a question, and say, 'Will those who are
saved ever think of the sins of which they were shriven here in their
lives, which they made clean, of which they were absolved?' Saint
Anselm answers this, and says that you who will have the bliss
of heaven will love God and thank him there for all goods, both large
and small, which he has done for you and for all others, in the
same way, who will be saved at the day of judgment and will have
endless bliss with you. He does great good for you, while you are
alive, when he forgives your sins. How then could you thank God
with a free heart for all he has forgiven you, all the sins you have
done, if you could not think of any of them?

It is at this point that he introduces the comparison to healed
wounds; a saved soul will remember the sins, but inasmuch as it has
been cleansed and forgiven, the remembrance will not be painful
but will rather be like a perfectly healed wound:

Bot þou salle þis understand wele,
Þat na mare grevance salle þou fele,
Ne na mare payne have, ne myslykyng,
When þou has of þi syns meneyng,
Þan he has, þat som tym had in stryfe

> A sare wound, with swerd or knyfe,
> Þat parfytely es haled and wele.

> But you must understand this well, that you will not feel any more
> grief or have any pain or disgust when you remember your sins
> than has a man who received a grievous wound in battle, with a
> sword or a knife, that has healed perfectly.

He then proceeds to his examples, saying that Peter has now no
shame for denying Christ, that Mary Magdalene has no shame for
the sins that once delighted her, and that the redeemed sing the
praises of God endlessly in accordance with the psalm of David,
another forgiven sinner:

> Þarfor says David, on þis manere:
> *Misericordiam Domini*
> *in eternum cantabo.*
> He says: 'I salle þe mercyes syng
> Of our Loverd, ay with-outen cesyng.'
> And swa salle alle syng, with-outen ende,
> Þat tylle þe blys of heven salle wende;
> And swa moght þai on nane wise syng,
> Warn þai had of þair syns meneyng,
> Þat þai had done here bodily
> And God forgaf thurgh his mercy.[18]

> Therefore David says, 'I shall sing the mercies of our Lord, always
> without ceasing.' And so shall all sing, endlessly, who shall go to the
> bliss of heaven. They could not sing thus unless they remembered
> their sins, which they did here in their bodies and which God forgave
> through his mercy.

The equation of sins and wounds and the belief in the possibility
of forgiveness would seem to make the link between healed wounds
and forgiven sins an obvious step within the *Gawain* poet's tradition. Patience tells Haukyn in *Piers Plowman* that

> satisfaccion sekeþ out þe roote, and boþe sleeþ and voideþ
> And as it neuere [n]adde ybe to noȝte bryngeþ dedly synne
> That it neuere eft is sene ne soor, but semeþ a wounde yheeled.[19]

Satisfaction seeks out the root and slays and annihilates deadly sin, as if it never had existed, so that it is never again visible or painful, but seems like a healed wound.

A similar discussion may be found in *Mirk's Festial*, in the sermon for Advent, in which it is suggested that the sins of which we have been shriven are a sign of honour, like the wounds a warrior has received in battle:

> as sone as he feleþe þat he hath synnet, anoon goo schryue bym, and mekly take þe dome of his schryft-fadyr: þen schall he haue yn þe day of dome gret remedy and worschip. For ryght as a knyght scheweth þe wondys þat he hath yn batayle, yn moche comendyng to hym; ryght so all þe synnys þat a man hath schryuen hym of, and taken hys penans for, schull be þer yschewet yn moch honowre to hym, and moche confucyon to þe fende. And þose þat haue not schryuen hom, hit schall be schowet to all þe world in gret confusyon and schenschyp.[20]

> As soon as he feels that he has sinned, let him go shrive himself at once, and take the judgment of his confessor. Then on the day of judgment he will have great remedy and honour. For just as a knight shows the wounds that he receives in battle, to his own praise, so all the sins that a man has confessed and received penance for will be displayed in great honour to him and to the confusion of the fiend. Those who have not confessed, it shall be revealed to all the world in great confusion and shame.

Gawain would like to use the green girdle as a sign for his own personal and permanent *untrawþ*. He is unsuccessful in this attempt, however, since he cannot establish it as a stable sign even for its first intended audience, the people of Arthur's court. This failure arises from the fact that the intended meaning is not something that is possible in the world of living humans: no living man is in a state of permanent *untrawþ*. The situation of Gawain at the end of the poem is that he is not in a state of grace but at any time until the moment of death he might always be restored to grace sacramentally. The appropriate sign for his condition is therefore not the pentangle of permanent Truth or the green girdle of permanent Untruth, for neither of these describes a human's condition properly until after the final judgment. When he is in a state of grace, as at the beginning of his adventure, the pentangle as the device on a Shield of Faith is his proper sign; once he has fallen, the correct sign for his cowardice is a wound, for wounds, like sin, may be healed. The green girdle, if it is to be a stable sign of anything, must signify *wanhope*.

5   Gawain as Exemplary Individual

As V.A. Kolve has said, in the general climate of medieval thinking about time, 'only one medieval conception of present time had an affirmative tone ... whatever else "now" might be, it was historically the time of mercy.'[1] As we have seen from the discussion in the previous chapter, authors in our period laid great stress on the fact that divine grace is now available for all those who are willing to achieve true repentance. Sermons and preaching handbooks are full of *exempla* that make this point clear through the fact of deathbed repentance: no matter how vicious a life has been, true contrition according to form at the last minute has been known to bring the sinner to salvation. The worst sin of all is to deny that this is possible; if the sinner himself denies it, he is guilty of *wanhope*, and if another person denies it, he is guilty of presumption, of claiming more knowledge of what is possible than God himself.

The difficulty with such stories and such a doctrine is that they imply, to a certain sort of mind, that the best course of action would be to sin as much and as enjoyably as possible until the last moment and then to partake of this escape from punishment as if by magic, confessing and repenting and making restitution before the moment of death. This problem is confronted and solved in various ways in all of the preaching handbooks current in the age. The author of *Jacob's Well* concentrates on two aspects of this strategy, pointing out first that, at the moment of death, dying people do not always have their wits about them, and secondly, that those who give alms after their death from their ill-gotten gains are attempting to deceive God by being charitable with other people's money:

But manye now in þise dayes faylen þis grace in syknes in here ende
for to haue parfyȝt sorwe, & desyre to be schreue, or dyspose hem
to makyn amendys. for þei abyde so longe, tyl here wyttes are gon, &
here resoun. deuocyoun haue þei non. here speche fayleth. here
dreed is go. speke to hem, styrre hem to gode, þey schewe no signe of
verray repentaunce, but lye stylle as a beste, wyth-oute swetnes &
dreed to godwarde & to here soule. Counseyle hem to restore here
dettys, here wrongys to þe cherch, to þe dede, or to þe qwyke, þat
will þei noȝt do. why? for þei haue no grace þerto. for, ȝif þei payeden,
& restoryd aȝen, þat þei haue falsly wyth-holdyn, þei schulde be
seuyd; þerfore þei wyll noȝt do so, to be sauyd, but þei robbyn seynt
Petyr, & ȝeuyn it seynt poule. þat þai falsely haue gettyn fro holy
cherch, fro here curatys, fro here neȝhbourys, þat schal noȝt be restoryd aȝen to hem þe same persones, but it schal be ȝouen to oþere
persones þat haue no skyl þerto, as to frerys & howsys of relygioun,
& to poore folk. so þat of oþere mennys good þou ȝeuyst þin almes
in þin ende, nouȝt to þe ownerys but to alyenis ... þis contricyoun in
þin ende & þin almes is a iape to god & damnacioun to þi soule.[2]

But many in these days in sickness at their ends lack this grace to
have perfect sorrow and the desire to be shriven or to dispose themselves to make amends. For they wait so long that their wits and
their reason are gone. They have no devotion. Their speech fails.
Their dread is gone. Speak to them, urge them to good, and they show
no sign of true repentance, but lie still as a beast, without sweetness
or dread towards God or their soul. Counsel them to repay their
debts, their wrongs to the church, to the living or the dead, they will
not do it. Why? Because they have no grace for it. For it they paid
and restored what they have falsely withheld, they would be saved;
therefore they will not do it, to be saved, but they rob Peter and
pay Paul. What they have got falsely from holy church, from their
curates, from their neighbours, that will not be restored by them to
the same persons but it will be given to other persons who have
no right to it, such as friars and houses of religion and poor people.
So that from other men's goods you give your alms in the end, not to
the owners but to strangers ... This contrition at your end and your
alms are an insult to God and damnation for your soul.

The author of the fourteenth-century *Book of Vices and Virtues*
points out the folly of persisting in a dangerous and wounded situa-

tion, and argues further that a man who delays penance runs a
great risk in that the hour of death is unknown to him:

> And þe wise seyn in holy writ, 'Ne tarie not, þat is a-bide not, to be
> schryue to God, ne drawe it not along bi excusacions from day to
> day, for þe abidyng in synne is wel perilous for many resouns.' First
> for þe self condicion of synne. For synne is wilde fier brennynge;
> þat ne may not be queynt but bi wepyng schrifte. A moche fool were
> he þat seiȝ his hous ofiere and ne wolde not renne to feche watre
> and he myȝt quenche it. And after, synne is ariȝt gret sekness, and þe
> schrift is þe medicine, and forsoþe he takeþ litle hede of his helþe
> þat wot hymself seke and in perel of deþ þat desireþ not to be heled.
> And after þis, þe deþ þat is nyȝh and þat ouer al awaiteþ þe synful
> man and woman scholde make hem bi resoun to go schryue hem
> hastiliche, for þei ne witen not þe poynt ne þe houre ne þe day þat
> deþ wole come, þat ofte and many tymes steleþ sodeynliche vpon þe
> synful whan he takeþ leste hede, and certes who-so wiste what
> deye he scholde deye he wolde haste to make hym redy þer-to.[3]

> And wise men say in holy writings, 'Do not tarry, that is, do not
> wait, to be confessed to God, and do not draw it out by excuses from
> day to day, for staying in sin is very dangerous for many reasons.'
> First, for the very condition of sin. Sin is a burning wild fire that may
> not be quenched except by weeping repentance. A man would be a
> great fool to see his house on fire and not run to fetch water to
> quench it if he could. Sin is also a very great sickness, and confession
> is the medicine, and truly he takes little heed for his health who
> knows himself sick and in peril of death and does not desire to be
> healed. Further, death that is near and awaits the sinful man and
> woman should make them, by reason, go to confess quickly, for they
> do not know the minute or the hour or the day when death will
> come, for it often steals suddenly upon the sinful man when he takes
> least heed, and certainly whoever knew the day he would die would
> hurry to make himself ready for it.

Both the *Speculum Sacerdotale*[4] and a sermon from ms Royal 18 B
xxiii make this same point, that 'þer is no þinge more certeyn
þan dethe, ne þer is no þinge more vncerteyn þan þe houre of dethe';
'There is nothing more certain than death and nothing more uncer-
tain than the hour of death.'[5] The most often-cited authority for
this kind of admonition is a sermon that was generally attributed to

Augustine, pointing out the great possibility of failure for those who plan late penance:

> Quanti enim qui se ad extremum vitae suae poenitentiam accepturos esse credebant, aut subita ruina oppressi, aut forte per naufragium demersi sunt, aut fulmine interfecti, aut sanguinis ictu, aut illa infirmitate quae apoplexia dicitur, ita percussi sunt; ut non solum poenitentiam petere, sed etiam signare se aut orationem Dominicam dicere omnino non possent?[6]

> How many men have there been who believed that they would receive penance at the end of their lives but then were overcome by a sudden fall, or perhaps drowned in a shipwreck, or were killed by lightning, or by a stroke of blood, or were so smitten by that disease that is called apoplexy that they were entirely unable to seek penance, or even to cross themselves or recite the Lord's Prayer?

In short, the risk is too great; the ploy of delaying penance until the moment of death will not work, so it is more sensible to prepare oneself now and to be always prepared for death:

> Man, þou wost wel þou shalt dyȝe;
> What deþ, ne where, þou nost whenne ...
> And sodeyn deþ nyl no man kenne.
> I rede we drede domesday;
> Be euene wiþ world er ȝe gon henne,
> ffor per schal be no iour delay.[7]

> Man, you know well that you will die, but you do not know what kind of death, or where, or when ... no man knows about sudden death, so I advise that we all fear doomsday. Be even with the world before you go away, for there will be no day of delay.

This general clerical strategy, which implies that the only thing wrong with this kind of calculation about deathbed conversion is its impracticability, is not spiritually very satisfying. What if it were possible to get away with it? If a man were somehow to determine the day of his death, he might be able to circumvent all the problems these authors foresee and have the best of both worlds: 'certes who-so wiste what day he scholde deye he wolde haste to make hym redy þer-to' (certainly whoever knew what day he was to die would make haste to be ready for it),[8] as the *Book of Vices and Virtues* says, or, in the words of Dan Michel, 'huo þet wyste huet day he ssolde sterue: he hine wolde agraypi ase zone ase he miȝte' (whoever knew what day he was to die would prepare himself for it as soon as he could).[9] The person who fantasizes about such a possibility, hoping to be able to circumvent the decrees of God, is clearly in a perilous state of soul, and the cool, reasoned arguments about the potential dangers of unexpected death can do little to remedy this. Some writers therefore turn to frightening threats, like the poet who quotes God as saying that the longer the sinner remains unrepentant, the greater will be his vengeance:

> ȝif man ligge long in synne,
> And wilfully fleeþ fro grace,
> To scharpe my wreche y wole bygynne,
> Take vengeaunce for his trespas.[10]

If a man lie long in sin and wilfully flees from grace, I will begin to sharpen my anger to take vengeance for his trespass.

The variety of techniques used to counteract the desire to delay repentance suggests that this was a serious problem in the period and that no one argument or threat was found to be sufficient to effect the Church's aims. As we might expect, the techniques used by the *Gawain* poet are considerably subtler than those used by the writers of sermons and manuals, but a comparison with this type of background material is essential for locating his efforts historically. Further, there is one preacher who used a device that helps immensely in shedding light on the poet's procedure. This man seems not to have been satisfied with rational arguments or threats of divine anger or unexpected accidents. Rather than argue, he resorts to vivid imagery to convey to his audience the belief that it is simply not possible to succeed in the delayed-repentance tactic. The particular image he chooses offers a striking connection to *Sir Gawain and the Green Knight*:

> Rubberes. and þa reueres. and þa þeoues. And þa morðslaȝa. and ȝitteres. and þa eawbrekeres. and þa liȝeres and þa wohdemeres and þa iuguleres. and þa oðer sottes alle heo habbeð an þonc fulneh. hwet seggeð heo. We moten idreȝan ure wil þe hwile þe we beoð ȝunge. and eft þenne we beoð eldre bete we hit þenne weilawei

wrecche. þus cweð þe boc. Soðliche al swa eða þu mihtest neoman
þine aȝen wepne and smiten of þin aȝen heaueð. and gan eft to
þin aȝene liche. hu mahtest þu gan to þine aȝene liche ȝif þin hefet
were offe. Nefre.[11]

'Robbers, spoilers, thieves, murderers, covetous, adulterers, liars,
unjust judges, jugglers, and other sots shall have a reward full
quickly.' What say they? We may follow our will while we are
young; and when we become older we will repent. Alas wretch! thus
saith the book, 'Forsooth as easily thou mightest take thine own
weapon and smite off thine own head and return again to thine own
likeness.' How mightest thou return to thine own likeness if thy
head were off? Never![12]

When the *Gawain* poet gives the Green Knight the power to perform
precisely this 'impossible' task, to come again to his own appearance
after his head has been cut off, he marks this story as one in which
we can expect other ordinary rules governing the world to be sus-
pended. It is not surprising that we find the other half of the preacher's analogy denied as well. Just as it is possible, in the world of
poem, for a severed head to be reattached, so it would seem possible
for Gawain to live his life as he pleases until the last day, and then
repent and be saved, for he, unlike other men, knows the day of his
death.

The technique the poet is using here is quite common in mythol-
ogical works. In order to show that particular types of behaviour
or values are unviable, especially in the case of a widespread suppressed longing to escape from rigorous social constraint, a supporter
of the social status quo takes the presuppositions of that suppressed
desire to their logical conclusion and embeds them in a narrative
that shows that the desire is either logically inconsistent or prag-
matically disastrous. In this case the poet is starting from the com-
monly held belief that the man who knew the day of his death
would be able to fulfil all his wishes (and, vicariously, those of his
audience) and then achieve perfect repentance on that day and so
win salvation. His narrative, however, shows that this is not the
case. Gawain is not able to sin gloriously throughout his year of
grace, for very soon after his appointment with death is made, the
oppressive fears begin to surround him. And, what is worse, he
is unable to repent and confess properly, not because of anything so
dramatic as a shipwreck or an apoplectic fit but because of his

simple desire to stay alive. Even the man who has been granted the knowledge of the day of his death is so attached to earthly life that he is willing to jeopardize his chance for endless spiritual joy in order to preserve it. If Gawain is to be seen as an example to the audience, part of the message is that all men, no matter how out-standing and no matter what special advantages they may be given, naturally put self-preservation and love of self higher than spiritual perfection.

B   GAWAIN'S USE OF EXEMPLARY FIGURES

The final section of Gawain's meeting with Bercilak at the Green Chapel is dominated by Gawain's 'anti-feminist' complaint against Lady Bercilak. Bercilak is attempting to bring about a final reconcili-ation, and he invites Gawain to return to the castle. Gawain refuses, politely but very firmly, and then proceeds to explain that he has been deceived, as many men in the past have been deceived by women:

> And comaundez me to þat cortays, your comlych fere,
> Boþe þat on and þat oþer, myn honoured ladyez,
> Þat þus hor knyȝt wyth hor kest han koyntly bigyled.
> Bot hit is no ferly þaȝ a fole madde,
> And þurȝ wyles of wymmen be wonen to sorȝe,
> For so watz Adam in erde with one bigyled,
> And Salamon with fele sere, and Samson eftsonez –
> Dalyda dalt hym hys wyrde – and Dauyth þerafter
> Was blended with Barsabe, þat much bale þoled.
> Now þise were wrathed wyth her wyles, hit were a wynne huge
> To luf hom wel, and leue hem not, a leude þat couþe.
> For þes wer forne þe freest, þat folȝed alle þe sele
> Exellently of alle þyse oþer, vnder heuenryche
>   þat mused;
> And alle þay were biwyled
> With wymmen þat þay vsed.
> Þaȝ I be now bigyled
> Me þink me burde be excused.   (2411–28)

And commend me to that courteous lady, your fair wife, and to both those honoured ladies, who have so skilfully deceived their knight with their strategem. But it is not to be wondered at if a fool behaves

madly and comes to grief through women's wiles. For here on earth
Adam was beguiled by one, and Solomon by many different women,
and Samson too – Delilah dealt him his doom – and later on David
was deceived by Bathsheba and suffered great misery. Now since
these were brought to grief by the wiles of women, it would be a
great gain to love them and never believe them, if a man could do it.
For these were the noblest men of ancient times, who were favoured
by fortune above all others who thought beneath the heavens. And
they were all beguiled by women that they had dealings with: though
I am now beguiled, I think that I ought to be excused.

This type of anti-feminist complaint, complete with biblical references, is widespread in our period, but the attitude it represents
is far from being universal. A contemporary poem called 'Of Women
cometh this Worldes Weal' uses some of the same examples but
goes on to say that much more evil has come into the world through
men:

Sum seiþ wimmen haþ be-gilt
Adam, Sampson and Salamon,
And seiþ þat wimmen haþ I-spilt
Many a wys worþi mon:
Þus þei greggen wymmens gilt;
Of Monnes riken þei neuer on.
And monnes falsehed weore fulfild,
I trowe þer weore twenti aȝeynes on,
Of Macabeus, Iudas and Ion,
Alisaundre and oþer feole,
Þat with monnes gult was fordon;
But of wimmen comeþ þis worldes wele.[13]

Some say that women beguiled Adam, Sampson, and Solomon and
that women have destroyed many a wise and worthy man. Thus they
complain about women's guilt, but pay no attention to men's. If
man's falsehood were counted up, I believe it would be twenty to one
– the Macabees, Judas and John, Alexander and many others who
were destroyed by man's guilt. But from women comes this world's
prosperity.

But perhaps more to the point here than the general acceptability
of Gawain's opinions about beguiling women is the question of

his purpose in referring to them.[14] The general context is the quasi-confessional scene with Bercilak, and at this point he is claiming that, since he has been beguiled as even the great men of the past have been beguiled, he ought to be excused: 'Me þink me burde be excused' (2428). Now this kind of self-absolution is universally condemned in the medieval period. Another poem from the Vernon manuscript says:

> 3if þou hast don aȝeyn god auis
> And after defendest hit I-wis,
> God is more greuet of þat defendyng
> Þen of þe furste sungyng.[15]

> If you have acted against good counsel and after defend yourself concerning it, God is more aggrieved by that defending than by the first sin.

The author of *Jacob's Well* insists that confession is the proper place for rehearsing one's own sins, not those of other people, and goes so far as to say that a confession that accuses other people becomes invalid:

> thynke of þin owen propre synnes & noȝt on oþere mennys. þerfore Ysaye seyth, xxxviij. 'Recogitabo tibi omnes annos meos' – non dicit alienos. I schal thynke to þe, god, alle myn ȝerys of synne; he seyȝt noȝt of oþerys ȝeris ... telle þin owne synnes, & noȝt þi neyȝbouris synnes; for [ȝif?] þi schryfte be noȝt hole of þin owen propyr synnes, but it is brokyn in-to oþer mennys synnes, it profyteth noȝt. þerfore, say þin owne synnes, late oþere mennys be! Ps. 'Dixi: confitebor aduersum me iniusticiam meam' – non dicit alienam.[16]

> think of your own sins and not of other men's. 'I will recount to thee, God, all my years of sin': he said nothing of others' years ... Tell your own sins, not your neighbour's sins, for if your confession is not completely of your own sins but is broken into by other men's sins, it does not profit. Therefore, tell your own sins, and let other men's be. As the Psalm says, 'I have said, I will confess against myself my injustice' – not other men's.

When reference is made to biblical precedents in the homiletic material of the period, the stress is on the importance of accepting the blame for one's own sin. *Jacob's Well* refers to David to make this point:

> Þe heued of þis scauel must be accusyng þi-self, noȝt excusyng þi-self in colouris, and putting þe defawte of þi synne on oþere persones, as þus; 'god ȝaf me no myȝt to with-stondyn it. oþere folk dyde me don it. It was oþerys defaute & noȝt myn. myn husbonde dede me don it, my wyif dyde me don it, or my wyif was cause þerof more þan I. temptacyouns & sterynges of oþere dyde me don it.' towche non oþer þan þi-self! make streyȝt þis heued & narow, þat it towche þi-self & non oþer! streyȝtly accuse þi-self & non oþer! as dauyd seyde to god, 'Ego peccaui,' I dyde þis synne of myn owen wyckydnes.[17]

> The head of this shovel must be accusing yourself, not excusing yourself with devices and putting the blame of your sin on other people, saying 'God gave me no power to withstand it' or 'other people made me do it' or 'it was others' fault and not mine' or 'my husband made me do it' or 'my wife made me do it' or 'my wife was more the cause of it than I' or 'temptations and urgings of others made me do it.' Touch no other than yourself. Make this head straight and narrow so that it touches you and no other. Accuse yourself straightly and no other. As David said to God, 'I have sinned,' I did this sin of my own wickedness.

The Book of Vices and Virtues argues the same way with the same exemplary figure, calling on the sinner to confess

> wiþ-oute any faire spekyng or forgynge or to make any excusaciouns or defences or to put any oþer in blame to excuse hymself wiþ, and so schrof hym David, þᵗ seiþ in pe Sauter, 'I wole schryue me and telle alle my synnes aȝens myself' and not aȝens oþere, as doþ ypocrites.[18]

> without any fair speaking or planning to make any excuses or defences or to put anyone else in blame in order to excuse himself, and so David confessed, as it says in the psalter, 'I will confess and tell all my sins against myself,' and not against others, as hypocrites do.

When there is a biblical character who does make use of the defence that another person caused him to sin, this excuse is treated as cause for blame:

> But doþ noʒt as many men doþ, scilicet, for to make ʒoure synnes whit and to gyldyn hem vnder excusatorie wordes and colours bi way of excusacion or of malys as dide Adam of Eue and as many men vsen this same day and here children also that foloweth hem in the same crafte. For thus answerd Adam what tyme that God reproued hym of his synne. And he seide thus to God: 'The womman,' he seide, 'þe whome þou ʒaue me mevyd me ther-to.' And also Eue excusid hure thus: 'The serpent,' sche seid, 'deceyued me and made me to ete.' For-þi do noʒt thus, for þen þou excusest þe noʒt, but thou accusest the. And ʒif thou wolt accuse thy-self, no doute it shall be to the verrey penaunce and reconciliation a-nense God.[19]

> But do not do as many men do, that is, make your sins white and gild them with excusing words and devices by way of excuse or malice, as Adam and Eve did and as many men do now, their children who follow them in the same wiles. For when God reproved him of his sin, Adam answered, 'The woman whom you gave me incited me to it.' And also Eve excused herself, saying 'The serpent deceived me and made me eat.' Therefore do not do this, for then you will not be excusing yourself, but accusing yourself. And if you will accuse yourself, no doubt it will be towards true penance and reconciliation with God.

But perhaps the best comparison text on this question is *Dives and Pauper*, which brings together the problem of self-excuse and the anti-feminist *exempla* and proceeds explicitly to destroy the ground of both. Dives claims that he would like to keep the sixth commandment but that women make it very hard for him. Pauper will have no part of such an attitude, and claims first that men deceive women more than women deceive men:

> DIUES Reson and holy write cachyn me to grantyn þat boþin auouterie & symple fornicacion ben wol greuous synnys, but mor greuous is auouterie & fayn Y wolde kepyn me from boþin synnys. But women ben þe fendis snaris & so temptyn men to lecherie þat it is wol hard to me for to kepyn me. Adam, Sampsonem, Petrum, Dauid & Salomonem femina decepit; quis modo tutus erit? Woman deceyuyd

Adam & Sampson, Petir, Dauyd & Salomon; ho may þan ben sykyr
from womanys gyle?
PAUPER Many man hat ben deceyuyd be wyckyd women mor be his
owyn folye þan be deceyt of woman, but many mo women han
ben deceyuyd be þe malyce of men þan euere wer men deceyuyd be
malice of woman.

DIVES Reason and holy writ caution me to grant that both adultery
and simple fornication are grievous sins, but adultery is more grievous, and I would like to keep myself from both sins. But women
are the fiend's snares and tempt me to lechery so much that it is very
hard for me to restrain myself. A woman destroyed Adam, Sampson,
Peter, David, and Solomon: who then will be safe from a woman's
guile?
PAUPER Many a man has been deceived by wicked women more by
his own folly than by deceit of women, but many more women have
been deceived by the malice of men than men were ever deceived
by the malice of women.

He then proceeds to demolish all of Dives' accusations against
women, case by case:

Þis fals excusacioun þat men so excusyn her synne be þe malyce of
woman began in Adam & les Adam & al mankende, for synfullyche
he excusyd hys synne be woman whan God vndrinam hym of hys
synne & putte woman in defaute; & also he put God in defaute
þat made woman & answered wol proudlyche, as men don þese dayys,
& seide to God: 'Woman þat þu ȝeue to me to ben myn felawe ȝaf
me of þe tre & Y eet perof,' as ho seye: Haddist þu nout ȝouyn hyr to
me to ben myn felawe Y schulde nout a synnyd. And so noutwith-
stondynge þat he was mor in defaute þan woman ȝet he wolde
nout knowlechyn ony defaute but he putte woman & God principaly
þat made woman in defaute.

This false excusing, in which men excuse their sin by the malice of
woman, began with Adam and destroyed Adam and all mankind,
for he sinfully excused his sin by woman when God reproved him for
his sin and he put the blame on woman. And also he put the blame
on God who made woman, and answered very proudly, as men do
these days, and said to God, 'The woman that you gave to me to be

my fellow gave me of the tree and I ate thereof,' as if to say, 'If
you had not given her to me to be my fellow, I would not have
sinned.' And so, notwithstanding that he was more to blame than the
woman, still he would not acknowledge any fault, but put woman
and especially God who made woman in blame.

And so Adam was deceyuyd & fallyn be pryde er Eue ȝaf hym þe
appyl, & Eue was deceyuyd be pryde er þe serpent deceyuyd hyr, for,
as seyth Sent Austyn, ubi supra [i.e., De civitate lib. xiv, x. xiii],
þey coueyteden mor excellence & heyere degre þan God ordeynyd
hem to.

And so Adam was deceived and fell through pride before Eve gave
him the apple, and Eve was deceived by pride before the serpent
deceived her, for as Saint Augustine says, they coveted more excellence and higher degree than God ordained for them.

DIUES But ȝit Y seye, as Y seyde first, woman deceyuyd Sampson þat
was so strong.
PAUPER Woman deceyuyd hym nout til he hadde deceyuyd hymself
be lecherie & mysgouernance of hymself.

DIVES But still I say as I said before, that a woman deceived Sampson
who was so strong.
PAUPER The woman did not deceive him until he had deceived
himself by lechery and misgovernance of himself.

Also Dauyd was deceyuyd be his myslust & his lecherie nout be þe
woman Bersabee ... Dauyd lokyd on þat woman in wil to don lecherye
whan þe woman þouȝte non euyl.

Also David was deceived by his lust and his lechery, not by the
woman Bathsheba ... David looked on that woman with a will to do
lechery, when the woman thought no evil.

Salamon souȝte þe companye of hethene women; the women wern
stable in her fals beleue, & he was vnstable in his ryȝth beleue &
folwyd her fals beleue & forsook Godys lawe in gret partye & wor-
chepyd false godys. Lecherye ouyrcam hym longe or many of þo
women knewyn hym.[20]

> Solomon sought the company of heathen women; the women were
> stable in their false belief, and he was unstable in his right belief,
> and followed their false belief and forsook God's law, in great part,
> and worshipped false gods. Lechery overcame him long before many
> of the women even knew him.

Gawain's outburst at this point is not to be criticized only as an
anti-feminist diatribe, for these were frequent enough in the poet's
age to become almost commonplace. Nor is it to be attacked on
merely chivalric grounds, although it does represent a real lapse in
the hero's courtesy, quite out of keeping with the rules of romance
literature. Rather, both the speech and the speaker are culpable
and even untrue, since the particular examples Gawain chooses do
not stand up to close scrutiny, and his whole intent, to excuse
himself from responsibility for his own lapse, is as sinful as the lapse
itself. This use of exemplary figures, as excuses for one's own faults,
is not permissible.

C   GAWAIN AS *EXEMPLUM*

There are two points of view from which we can consider the
problem of the poet's purpose in presenting his audience with a story
about a man who is first displayed as humanly perfect and then
shown to be, in reality, seriously flawed. In the historical context it
must be seen against the background of beliefs about the way in
which we are to interpret the fact that man was created in God's
image. In the context of the poem itself we must decide about the
proper response to the story of the fall of a great man. Despite the
fact that the poem's internal audience uses Gawain's fall just as he
uses the fall of biblical heroes, the poet expects his own audience
to respond in a more productive way.

The latter part of the fourteenth century in England was a time of
great concern over idols and idolatry. It seemed to many that the
Christian use of representations of the cross, of Christ, of the Virgin,
and of the saints was a violation of the first commandment, which
forbids the worshipping of graven images. In the early years of
the century these objections seem not to have been too strong and
required only brief treatment from the defenders of images. Richard
Rolle, for example, needs only a few words to deal with the problem
of reverence for crosses:

Haly crosses men sall lowte, For thay are in syngne of Cryste crucy-
fiede. To images es þe louynge þat es till thaym of whaym þaire
are þe ymageȝ; For þat Entent anely þaire are for to lowte.[21]

Men shall honour holy crosses, for they are a sign of Christ crucified.
The honour that goes to images is to those of whom they are the
images, and they are to be honoured only with that purpose.

Some years later, it was still possible even for Wyclif to accept
images as part of Christian worship, although he is more concerned
about the possibilities of abuse and goes into greater detail about
the state of mind with which to approach this image. He quotes with
approval St Gregory's assertions that images may be used as books
for instruction of the illiterate and that they cause the minds of
those who see them to turn to deeper devotion. As long as the image
functions to these ends, there is no violation of the first commandment, but otherwise the practice leads to idolatry:

Et patet quod ymagines tam bene quam male possunt fieri: bene ad
excitandum, facilitandum et accendendum mentes fidelium, ut
colant devocius Deum suum; et male ut occasione ymaginum a veritate fidei aberretur, ut ymago illa vel latria vel dulia adoretur, vel
ut in pulcritudine, preciositate aut affecione impertinentis circum-
stancie minus debite delectetur.

And it is clear that images can work as much for good as for ill, since
they work well for arousing, aiding, and inciting the minds of the
faithful so that they may more devoutly honour their God; and evilly
as, by the occasion of images, he may be led astray from the truth
of faith, as the image is adored either through 'latria' or 'doulia,' or is
loved for its beauty, value, or for affection of some completely
unsuitable circumstance.

The ground of the error of idolatry, Wyclif says, is the confusion
between the sign and its referent:

Cum ergo primo et maximo mandato precipimur non adorare hu-
manam fabricam, in tantum quod Iudei precipiuntur non facere tales
ymagines, patet quod summa diligencia cavere debemus venenum
sub melle adorando ydolatrice signum loco signati.[22]

Since therefore we are ordered by the first and greatest commandment not to adore human fabrication, inasmuch as the Jews were ordered not to make such images, it is clear that we must, with greatest diligence, avoid the poison beneath the honey of adoring in idolatrous fashion the sign in place of the referent.

In his writing on the Eucharist, Wyclif takes the argument a stage further. He argues that just as the veneration of images and relics is permissible only if one is able to bypass their physicality in devotion to the creator ('suspendere consideracionem signi sensibilis et appendere totam intencionem et affectionem in creatore ymaginis'), in the same manner as a clerk pays attention to meaning rather than to physical writing, so too the adoration of the host is proper only if one honours through it the humanity of Christ:

> Sed nimis multi sunt layci et bestiales sensilibus nimium intendentes et multi, ut loquitur Apostolus Iᵃ Cor. XIIᵒ, 2, cum adorando hostiam *tanquam gentes ad simulacra muta prout decebantur captivi euntes* ad ydolatrandum sicut brutum ad iugum servilis operis. Qui autem adorat humanitatem Cristi ut talem in hostia, adorat in ipsa Christum yperdulia, et nemo rite adorat ipsam sub racione propria.

> But there are too many laymen and men too attentive as animals to their senses, and many, as the Apostle says in First Corinthians 12:2, who, when adoring the host, 'like gentiles are led captive to mute images,' to idolatry, like an animal to the yoke of the work of servitude. Who adores the humanity of Christ as such in the host adores Christ in it by 'hyperdulia,' and no one correctly adores it for its own sake.

The logical conclusion he feels compelled to draw from this is that since man was created in the image of God, man is more to be honoured than the host:

> et sic vere concluditur quod homo sit multiplicius honorandus quam hostia et adorandus tanquam ymago Dei, vas virtutum et sic Christus, verius quam hostia consecrata.[23]

And so it is truly concluded that man is much more to be honoured

than the host and to be adored as an image of God, a vessel of
virtues, and thus as Christ, more truly than the consecrated host.

The idea that man is a better image of God than anything else does
not play a great part in Wyclif's thought, nor is it original with
him, since similar statements can be found in orthodox works and
even in the writings of the Fathers.[24] Nevertheless, in the succeeding
years, as Lollard criticism of the orthodox use of images develops,
we find this point argued forcefully and even treated as a touchstone
of Lollard doctrine. In the first full extant statement of the tenets
of Lollard belief, the conclusions presented to Parliament in 1395, it
is a fully formed article. The eighth conclusion not only condemns
the veneration of relics by a striking *reductio ad absurdum* but also
argues that the expenses paid for wooden and stone images would
be better used as alms for men, the true images of God:

> Þe viii. conclusiun nedful to telle to þe puple be gylid is þe pilgrimage,
> preyeris, and offringis, made to blynde rodys and to deue ymages
> of tre and of ston, ben ner of kin to ydolatrie and fer fro almesse
> dede. And þow þis forbodin ymagerie be a bok of errour to þe lewid
> puple, ȝet þe ymage usuel of Trinite is most abhominable. Þis
> conclusiun God opinly schewith, comanding to don almesse dede to
> men þat ben nedy, for þei ben þe ymage of God in a more liknesse
> þan þe stok or þe ston, for God seyth nout, 'Faciamus lignum ad
> ymaginem et similitudinem nostram aut lapidem,' but 'Faciamus
> hominem etc.' For þe heye worchipe þat clerkis clepin 'latria' longith
> to þe Godhead alone, and þe lowere worchipe þat is clepid 'dulia'
> longith to man and to aungel and to lowere creatures. Þe correlari is,
> þat þe seruise of þe rode, don twyes every ȝer in oure Chirche, is
> fulfillid of ydolatrie, for if þe rode tre, naylis, and þe spere, and þe
> coroune of God schulde ben so holiche worchipid, þanne were Iudas
> lippis, qwoso mythte hem gete, a wondir gret relyk. But we preye
> þe, pilgrym, us to telle qwan þu offrist to seyntis bonis enschrinid in
> ony place, qweþir releuis þu þe seynt þat is in blisse, or þe pore
> almes hous þat is so wel enduwid. For men ben canonizid, Got wot
> how, and for to speken more in playn, trewe Cristemen supposin
> þat þe poyntis of þilk noble man, þat men clepin seynt Thomas, were
> no cause of martyrdom.[25]

The eighth conclusion that must be told to the beguiled people is
that the pilgrimages, prayers, and offerings made to blind roods and

deaf images of tree and stone are near akin to idolatry and far
from almsgiving. Though this forbidden imagery is a book of error to
the common people, yet the customary image of the Trinity is
most abominable. God shows this conclusion openly, commanding
us to give alms to men who are needy, for they are the image of
God in a greater likeness than the stock or the stone, for God did not
say, 'Let us make wood or stone after our image and likeness,' but
'Let us make man ...' For the high worship that clerks call 'latria'
belongs to the Godhead alone, and the lower worship that is called
'doulia' belongs to man and angels and lower creatures. The corrolary
is that the service of the rood, done twice each year in our church,
is filled with idolatry. For if the rood tree, nails, spear, and the crown
of God should be worshipped in such holiness, then if someone
could get Judas's lips, they would be a marvellous relic. But we pray
you, pilgrim, to tell us, when you make offering to saints' bones
enshrined in any place, whether you are relieving the saint, who is in
bliss, or the poor alms house, that is so well endowed. Men are
canonized, and only God knows how; and to speak more plainly, true
Christian men believe that the qualities of that noble man whom
people call Saint Thomas were no cause for martyrdom.

The *Apology for Lollard Doctrine*, which passed under the name of
Wyclif, offers a similar criticism of image worship and a similar
substitute:

> If ymagis be worschipid, not bi vicary worschip, but by þe same
> worschip of God, doutles it is idolatrie; for noiþer þe stok, noiþer þe
> craft of man is to be worschipid so. It is certeyn bi witnes of holy
> writ, and of seyntis, and of experiens, þat we awe not to arett swelk
> þingis, or þingis formid of mannis craft, heyar nor euen to man in
> kynd, wam God haþ maad to his ymage and similitude; ne we owe
> not to rett hem more lek to Crist, or to seyntis, in form or represen-
> tacoun, þan man, ne worþiar ne holyar gostly; ne we howe not to
> hope ne trist in hem more, ne luf hem better; ne ȝef hem moo þingis,
> ne grace. God biddiþ vs honor man many fold, and for many causes;
> and it is not were he biddiþ so worschip þer ymages, but his forbeding
> to worschip hem is opunly found.[26]

> If images are worshipped, not by vicarious worship but by the same
> worship as God, doubtless it is idolatry. For neither the stock nor
> the craft of man is to be so worshipped. It is certain, by witness of

Scripture, of saints, and of experience, that we ought not to consider such things, or any things formed by man's craft, higher or even equal to man in nature, whom God has made to his image and likeness. Nor should we consider them more like Christ or the saints, in form of representation, than man, nor worthier nor spiritually more holy. We ought not to hope or trust in them more, nor love them better, nor give them more things or grace. God bids us honour man in many ways and for many reasons, and there is no place where he bids us do worship to images, but his injunction against worshipping them is openly found.

This complaint persisted into the time of Reginald Pecock, who quotes the following argument from contemporary Lollards:

Vein and waastful occupacioun it is forto make myche labour and cost forto haue and vse the sympler and vperfiter and lasse representing ymage of a thing, whanne with lasse labour and cost mai be had the perfiter and fuller and better representing ymage of the same thing. But so it is, that ech lyuyng man is verier and perfiter and fuller and better representing ymage of Christ and of ech Seint, then is eny vnquyk stok or stoon graued and ourned with gold and othere gay peinturis. Wherefore it is vein and waast forto make such labour and cost into the making and hauyng of such vnquyke gay ymagis.[27]

It is a vain and wasteful occupation to make much labour and cost to have and use a simpler and less perfect and less representative image of a thing when with less labour and cost the more perfect and fuller and more representative image of the same thing may be found. But so it is that every living man is a truer and fuller and more representative image of Christ and every saint than is any lifeless stock or stone carved and adorned with gold or other gay painting. Therefore it is vain and a waste to expend such labour and cost to make and have such lifeless gay images.

This opinion was by no means limited to theoretical discussions between Lollards and orthodox critics but is found frequently in the records of legal proceedings against individuals charged with heresy.[28]

It seems clear, on the basis of the arguments discussed in an earlier chapter concerning the difference between divine perfection and human perfection, that complaints like these would not find

a great deal of support in orthodox circles. While all Christian writers
believe that man was created in God's image, nevertheless this
does not make each individual human a sign for God in the same
way that a picture is a sign for its subject. But we do not need to rely
on inferences from statements made on other topics, since the
orthodox defenders of images were quite clear on this particular
subject and dealt with it in a way that casts light on *Sir Gawain and
the Green Knight.*

In dealing with the heretical opinions of the Lollards generally and
with their iconoclasm in particular, orthodox writers could draw
on arguments and proof texts from past controversies for most of
their points. It is not surprising to find them using the same biblical
passages dealing with divinely approved images set up by Moses
and Solomon, the same legends about portraits of Christ painted in
his own lifetime, and the same authorities as were used by Byzantine
iconophiles some seven centuries earlier.[29] The insistence of the
Lollards that man is the only true image of God, however, was
something new, an idea not central to the argument of the Byzantine
iconoclasts, perhaps because they believed in the real presence in
the Eucharist. It was therefore necessary for each anti-Lollard writer
to make creative use of other material available to him from various
sources to counteract this argument. Just as the heresy is particularly fourteenth-century English, so too will be at least this portion
of orthodox reaction.

The defenders of images seem to agree that man is made unsuited
to honour as an image of God because of certain characteristics he
possesses in addition to the fact that he was created in the image of
God. Thomas Netter, for example, uses ordinary human perception
as an analogy:

> Unde si oculus vel aer esset de se coloratus, non reciperet aliquam
> coloris speciem per sui medium transferendam ac sensum; sed
> suo colore sensum afficeret: & ideo quanto est ab omni colore remo-
> tior, tanto est aptius medium visibili repraesentando. Ita & imago
> illa est aptius repraesentivum Dei, aut hominis ad mentem colentis,
> & susceptivum instrumentum divini cultus, quo est a vita, ratione,
> aut excellenti manifestatione ejus congrua saltem proportione
> remotius.[30]

Therefore if the eye or the air were itself coloured, it would not
receive any type of colour to be transferred through it to the sense,

but it would affect the sense by its colour. And so, the more it is remote from every colour, the more appropriate it is as a medium for representing the visible. So also the image is more appropriate as a representation of God, or better for the mind of a believing human, and an appropriate instrument of divine worship, in exact proportion as it is remoter from life or reason or from its precise manifestation.

From this point of view an image such as the pentangle is more appropriate as a sign for God than is a man, since it is transparently a sign, without other qualities that colour or distort the referent it signifies, whereas a particular man, even an excellent man like Gawain, is not sufficiently 'colourless' to be a serviceable image of God.

Reginald Pecock sees other problems with using an individual man as a sign for God. Quite apart from the fact that man was not made to be a sign for God in the first place, man is not properly designed to serve the function of an image at all. His presence provokes many other types of thoughts in one who sees him, so that he is a reminder of too many things to be an appropriate sign for any one thing:

> The iij^e. condicioun is, that the thing so deputid forto represente to us the othir thing, haue not (at leest for thilk while) eny plites or officis or deputaciouns or disposiciouns, wherbi we must haue eny othere entermetingis with him than the entermeting of remembring oonli; and that he haue not with us eny entermetingis saue the entermeting of representing oonli. Forwhi, if the thing which is deputid forto represente to us an other thing be such that we haue manye vsis of it and many entermetingis with it dyuers fro remembring bi it the othir thing, oure witt schall falle so miche and so ofte vpon the same thing in othere wisis than as he is representing the other thing, that he schal seelde among be occupied of us as representing the othir thing.

> The third condition is that the thing chosen to represent the other thing to us must not have, at least for the time, any roles, functions, or dispositions whereby we would have any other connections with it than the connection of remembering only, and it must not have any connection with us other than the connection of representing. For if the thing that is chosen to represent another thing to us be such that we have many uses for it and many other connections

with it other than remembering the other thing by it, our mind
will fall so much and so often on the same thing in other ways than
as it is representing the other thing that it will seldom be understood
by us as representing the other thing.

This is the case, quite obviously, with any living person, all of
whom perform so many other functions and call our minds to so
many other associated ideas that they cannot be efficient reminders
of any single referent:

> Wherefore no man lyuyng and walking in erthe and occupiyng him
> silf and occupied of othere men, as othere men lyuen and walken and
> occupien and ben occupied, is so perfit and so ful an ymage of Crist
> crucified or of Crist doing this miracle or that myracle, as graued
> stok or stoon therto schapun is.[31]

> Therefore, no man living and walking on earth and occupying himself
> and occupied with other men, as other men live and walk and
> occupy and are occupied, is so perfect and so complete an image of
> Christ crucified or of Christ doing this miracle or that miracle,
> as a graven stock or stone that is fashioned for that purpose.

The stone image, simply because it is lifeless, is a more apt image of
its divine referent than any living man could be.

Roger Dymmok makes use of similar arguments, but he adds one
drawn from considerations of everyday life and ethics. He considers
what would happen to a man who was treated with the honour
due to an image of God, and decides that the consequences are
unacceptable:

> si homo hominem adoraret adoracione latrie, cum homo ex se
> creatura sit racionalis et dignus honore, posset quis estimare latriam
> deberi homini exhiberi, et sic talis adoracio posset esse introductio
> ydolatrie, et similiter homo, cui fieret talis honor, ex hoc posset erigi
> in superbiam. Non sic autem de ymagine mortua, de qua constat,
> quod in se nullo honore est digna, nec in sua estimacione eleuari po-
> test aut deprimi, cum nec sentire possit nec intelligere. Ex quibus
> patet racio diuersitatis de latria exhibenda ymagini Christi depicte et
> non ymagini uiue Dei, id est, homini.[32]

> If man were to adore man with the adoration of 'latria,' although

man is in himself a rational creature and worthy of honour, someone
would think that 'latria' ought to be offered to man, and so such
an adoration could be the beginning of idolatry, and similarly the
man to whom such honour came could be raised into pride from
this. It is not the same with a lifeless image, concerning which it is
agreed that in itself it is worthy of no honour, nor could it be raised
or lowered in its own estimation since it is able neither to feel nor
to understand. From this is clear the rationale for the contradiction
that 'latria' is to be shown to the painted image of Christ and not
to the living image of God, that is, to man.

The late date of these writings, a few years after our manuscript of
Sir Gawain and the Green Knight, should by no means be taken
as an indication that the problem they confront and the manner of
their solution arose after the poem was written. It is rather a result
of the unavailability of written records of a debate that was being
carried on, both within the universities and outside, during the last
decades of the fourteenth century, and was simply one of the focal
points for two opposing currents in English thought pre-dating the
Lollard controversy by many years. Anne Hudson, in her notes to
an edition of a Lollard tract on images and pilgrimages, gives evidence
that the question of images was a matter for contention even prior
to the decisive conflict between Wyclif and the ecclesiastical hierarchy; unfortunately, many of the texts to which she refers remain
unpublished:

> Though the refusal of honor to images of saints, and the associated
> disrespect for pilgrimages, came to be perhaps the commonest Lollard
> beliefs, these two questions were apparently under discussion before
> Wyclif. Woodford, later an ardent opponent of Wyclif, discussed
> the matters in his *Postilla super Matthaeum* dating from 1372-3 (CUL
> MS Additional: I 3571, ff. 117, 119v–122), and it is clear from this
> that many of the arguments were already well-worn (see J.I. Catto,
> *William Woodford*, O.F.M. (c. 1330–c. 1397) (unpub. Oxford D. Phl.
> thesis, 1969), pp. 150–55). Although a number of points go right
> back to the eighth-century iconoclastic controversy of the eastern
> church (see E. R. Harvey, *The Inward Wits* ... (unpub. London Ph.D.
> thesis, 1970), pp. 179 ff.), the use of scholastic terminology and of
> contemporary examples shows that the matters must have been de-
> bated in the late fourteenth-century schools.[33]

After a list of similar manuscripts on the topic, Hudson points out

that there is sufficient overlap between the various treatises to
suggest an ongoing debate and that words had given way to actions
as early as 1382, when Lollards began destroying images.

It does not seem at all far-fetched to me to suggest that the
Gawain poet is involved, on the orthodox side, in this debate, especially with regard to the question of the ways in which an individual
man is the image of God. His heroes, like the dreamer in *Pearl* and
Jonah in *Patience*, are fallible men, not perfect ones. Nor is his
Gawain in any way comparable to a Galahad, as in the thirteenth-
century *Queste del Saint Graal*, for Galahad is incapable of error.

With the debate over images as background, it is possible to see
the history of Gawain as a comment on the question of the proper
image of God. The passage describing the pentangle establishes
that the device is an appropriate sign for the honourable, endless
perfection of Truth. It then suggests that Gawain is, at that moment,
to be associated with Truth, and that he too should be honoured.
It might seem, to a member of the audience influenced by the hu-
manist tendencies animating the Lollard view of man as an image of
God, that Gawain is more to be honoured at the moment of his
departure from Camelot than any graven symbol, such as a pentangle.
He is alive, in a state of grace, and was created in God's image; the
pentangle is lifeless, performs no actions at all, and was created
as a symbol by men, not by God.

But the unfolding of the story shows that it would be a mistake,
from the orthodox point of view, to see him this way. Gawain
'represents' too many other things to be an appropriate sign for God.
He is individualized for us, and we become interested in his particular strengths and weaknesses; and it becomes very difficult to see
him only as an image for something else, even if we see him as a
representative of fallible humanity. The Truth with which we con-
nect him is present in him only as faith, and even his faith is fragile
and easily shattered. Reverence for such a man is not only incorrect;
it is positively dangerous, since it can lead both to pride and to its
mirror image, the despair of ever being whole again that Gawain
displays at the end of the poem. From this point of view humanism
is next to idolatry.

D   THE LESSONS OF THE FALL

If contemporary orthodoxy would prevent us from offering to an
ordinary mortal the honours due to a perfect being because of the
dangers of idolatry, we must look elsewhere to discover the appro-

priate attitude towards Gawain and his story. Even if we were
tempted to give him such honours in the early part of the poem, the
affair at Bercilak's castle and his subsequent mischance at the Green
Chapel make it clear that Gawain is not perfect; perhaps, then, it
is precisely his fall from grace that makes him an apt focus for the
human characteristics that the poet wishes to examine. If this is
the case, the proper starting-point for a historicist study is an examination of contemporary attitudes towards the generally virtuous
man who breaks his circle of perfection by a moral lapse.

Gawain's own attitude towards such stories has already been
studied. He uses the narratives of the lapses of Adam, Solomon,
Samson, and David as support for his belief that he should be par-
doned for his fault, since men as excellent as these have also fallen
by the deceit of women. This scene not only contributes to the
characterization of Gawain but also provides a possible model for
audience response to Gawain's own adventures and predicament. The
poem as a whole (at least up to the last few stanzas) can easily be
read as providing an excuse for the flaws in a member of the audience: Gawain's fall shows that perfection is simply too high a goal
for an ordinary human, and so we too should be excused for our
flaws. This is, in effect, what is done by the poem's internal audience,
Arthur's courtiers at Camelot.

But the inclusion of this internal audience serves to undermine
the possibility of such a response in the reader. The court's trivializ-
ing reaction to Gawain's claim to be eternally untrue comes as a
bit of a surprise if the serious tone of the intervening lines has led
us to forget that the courtiers were first presented to us as lost
in childish and unthinking mirth. Their response to his gloomy and
despairing opinion that his stain is irremediable is an outburst of
laughter quite out of keeping with the mood of the preceding stanzas:

> Þe kyng comfortez þe knyȝt, and alle þe court als
> Laȝen loud þerat, and luflyly acorden
> Þat lordes and ladis þat longed to þe Table,
> Vche burne of þe broþerhede, a bauderyk schulde haue,
> A bende abelef hym aboute of a bryȝt grene,
> And þat, for sake of þat segge, in swete to were.
> For þat watz acorded þe renoun of þe Rounde Table,
> And he honoured þat hit hade euermore after. (2513–20)

The king comforted the knight, and all the court also laughed loudly

at it and amiably agreed that the lords and the ladies that belonged
to the Round Table, each man of the brotherhood, should wear a
baldric, crosswise around him, of bright green, and wear it thereafter
for the sake of that man, for that was considered the renown of
the Round Table, and he who had it was honoured ever after.

The poet is displaying in narrative form the feeling of confusion
created by all courts instituted by fallen humans, with their incom-
prehensible attitudes and topsy-turvy sense of moral values: a badge
symbolizing man's frailty, that the hero uses as a sign of permanent
sinfulness, becomes by fiat a sign of the renown of the Round
Table and a token of honour for the greatest group of knights in
Christendom. The situation is reminiscent of Walter Map's bewil-
derment in the face of his court:

> *In tempore sum et de tempore loquor*, ait Augustinus, et adiecit:
> *nescio quid sit tempus.* Ego simili possum admiracione dicere quod
> in curia sum, et de curia loquor, et *nescio, Deus scit,* quid sit curia.
> Scio tamen quod curia non est tempus; temporalis quidem est,
> mutabilis et uaria, localis et erratica, *nunquam in eodem statu per-
> manens.* In recessu meo totam agnosco, in reditu nichil aut modicum
> inuenio quod deliquerim; extraneam uideo factus alienus ... Si quod
> Boecius de fortuna veraciter asserit de curia dixerimus, recte quidem
> et hoc, *ut sola sit mobilitate stabilis.* Solis illis curia placet qui
> graciam eius consecuntur. Nam et ipse *gracias dat*: non enim ama-
> biles aut merentes amari diligit, sed indignos uita gracia sua donat.
> Hec est enim gracia que sine racione uenit, que sine merito considet,
> que causis occultis adest ignobilis. *Mistica uannus* Domini iudicio
> vero, iusta ventilacione sibi segregat a zizania frumentum: hec
> non minori sollicitudine sibi separat a frumento zizaniam: quod illa
> prudenter eligit hec inprudenter eicit, et e conuerso, sicut et in
> quampluribus.[34]

'I am in time, and I speak of time,' said Augustine, and straightway
added, 'I know not what time is.' With like wonderment can I say
that I am in the court, and speak of the court, and know not – God
alone knoweth – what the court is. This I know withal that the
court is not time; it partaketh, indeed, of time's temper, a thing of
flux and change, of a place, yet of subtle shifts, 'never persisting
in the same subsistence.' At my withdrawal from it, I know it through
and through; on my return to it, I find little or nothing that I have

left there; having become a stranger I view it as a thing altogether strange ... If what Boethius asserteth truthfully of fortune, we shall say of the court, our saying, indeed, will be right in this too, 'that it alone is constant in its change.' The court pleaseth only those who attain its favour, for it giveth favour arbitrarily; it doth not indeed love the lovable or those deserving to be loved, but presenteth those unworthy of life with its favour. For this is the favour which cometh without reason, which abideth without desert, and which aideth the ignoble, for reasons that do not appear. As 'the mystical fan' of God, by true judgment, by just winnowing, separateth for its own purpose the wheat from the chaff, so this fan of the court, with no less care, separateth for its purpose the chaff from the wheat: what the first wisely chooseth, the second unwisely casteth out, and conversely, as very often happeneth.[35]

Arthur's court, at this point in the narrative, 'for its purpose' prefers a fallen Gawain to a perfect or perfectible Gawain, prefers the chaff to the wheat. By adopting his badge of shame as a badge of honour, the courtiers are forestalling any criticism of themselves by referring their accusers to Gawain's fall as proof that no one is capable of meeting the standards of divine perfection.

This is perhaps not precisely the same thing as self-excuse for a particular lapse, but it comes perilously close, and it arises from comparable attitudes towards sin in general and a comparable technique of interpreting tales of great sinners. It is clear that this type of misuse of stories of the lapses of virtuous people was well known to the Fathers, since discussions of David's sin with Bathsheba, attached to expositions of his song of repentance in Psalm 50(51), often deal with the contrasting responses of the virtuous and the sinful towards their own lapses. Cassiodorus contrasts the attitude of the general crowd with that of the powerful king:

> Vulgo mos est peccata sua callidis allegationibus excusare; rex autem potentissimus in conspectu omnium se potius eligit addicere: constituens se reum, cuius consueuerat populus formidare iudicium. Quapropter ideo a domino absolui meruit, quoniam sua uitia non defendit.[36]

> The custom of ordinary people is to excuse their own sins with crafty allegations, but the most powerful king chose rather to accuse himself in the sight of it all; he whose judgment the people used to

dread declared himself to be guilty. Therefore he was worthy of being absolved by God, since he did not defend his sinful acts.

Augustine addresses those who make improper use of the story of David, again pointing out that David himself did not act in this way:

> Multi enim cadere volunt cum David, et nolunt surgere cum David. Non ergo cadendi exemplum propositum est, sed si cecideris, resurgendi. Attende, ne cadas. Non sit delectatio minorum lapsus majorum, sed sit casus majorum tremor minorum ... Audiunt male audientes, et quaerunt sibi patrocinia peccandi; attendunt unde defendant quod committere paraverunt, non unde caveant quod non commiserunt, et dicunt sibi: Si David, cur non et ego? Inde anima iniquior, quae cum propterea fecerit quia David fecit, ideo pejus quam David fecit ... Hoc amas in David, quod in se odit David: praeparas te ad peccandum, disponis peccare: librum dei ut pecces inspicis.[37]

> For many men will to fall with David, and will not to rise with David. Not then for falling is the example set forth, but if thou shalt have fallen for rising again. Take heed lest thou fall. Not the delight of the younger be the lapse of the elder, but be the fall of the elder the dread of the younger ... These men hear that are ill hearers, and seek for themselves countenance for sinning: they look out for means whereby they may defend what they have made ready to commit, not how they may beware of what they have not committed, and they say to themselves, If David, why not I too? Thence that soul is more unrighteous, which, forasmuch as it hath done it because David did, therefore hath done worse than David ... Thou dost love that in David, which in himself David hated: thou makest thee ready to sin, thou inclinest to sin: in order that thou mayest sin thou consultest the book of God.[38]

Augustine's statement describes and condemns the attitude of Arthur's court towards Gawain and his fall. They reveal that they 'love that in Gawain which Gawain hates' by adopting his green girdle of shame as a symbol of their own renown. This is an implicit claim that they deserve to be excused for whatever sins they may have committed or will commit in the future. In effect they are using the story of Gawain to avoid responsibility for their own actions, just as he used the stories of David and the other virtuous men of the Bible. Similarly, the poem as a whole challenges its audience to choose between two possible responses. We may either say 'If Gawain, why not I too?' or we may hear to our health by concentrating not on the fall but on the possibilities of rising again through true repentance.

A further dimension to this parallel with scriptural virtuous men emerges from the contrast between the nature of the lapse we expect from Gawain during his encounters with Lady Bercilak and the error that he actually commits. As the scene is unfolding, we expect Gawain to imitate the fall of David, since he seems about to take another man's wife. But in the event the nature of his fall is quite different. Despite the fact that he has set himself up as the pentangle knight, the type of Christian perfection, he ends up by placing his trust not in God or the Virgin but in his own devices, and is untrue to his covenant in order to save his own life. The virtuous man whose lapse he does finally imitate is Peter, who, despite his proud claim that he would never deny Christ even if it meant death (Matt 26:35), denied him three times when danger threatened. But both the story of David and the story of Peter are narrated, we are told, for the same purpose. Gregory the Great's explanation, in a passage quoted also in the *Glossa Ordinaria*, could serve as an epigraph for *Sir Gawain and the Green Knight*:

> Ad hoc quippe in Scriptura sacra virorum talium, id est David et Petri, peccata sunt indita, ut cautela minorum sit ruina majorum. Ad hoc vero utrorumque illic et poenitentia insinuatur et venia, ut spes pereuntium sit recuperatio perditorum. De statu ergo suo David cadente, nemo superbiat. De lapsu etiam David surgente, nemo desperet. Ecce quam mirabiliter Scriptura sacra eodem verbo superbos premit, quo humiles levat.[39]

> For the sins of such persons, that is, of David and Peter, are recorded in Scripture for this end, that the fall of their betters may be a caution to inferiors. But the penitence and the pardon of both are alike inserted to this end, that the recovery of the lost may be the hope of the perishing. Let no one boast then of standing firm himself, when David falls. Let no one also despair of his own rise, when David rises. Behold how marvellously Holy Scripture humbles the proud with the same word with which it raises up the humble.[40]

If we were to remain at the level of the poem as artifact, as a work in isolation, we would be left with an unresolved conflict. Gawain's view of his own actions is that they have removed him permanently from a state of grace and any possibility of attaining perfection. The court, however, seem to be treating his lapse as something trivial and his response to it as something far out of proportion. We might of course resolve this conflict on the level of personal predilection, but this is an approach at odds with the method undertaken here. We are left with the possibility of resolving it through analysis of the varius levels of meaning pointed out in the introduction.

Gawain is attempting, at the level of pure signification, to make the green girdle a sign for endless *untrawþ*. It might be accepted as such, but it is placed into a context that makes this impossible: no living human being is inescapably untrue, so the green girdle cannot stand for Gawain's permanent *untrawþ*. The green girdle fails also at the level of its effect on the minds of its audience. It does not cause them to think of the idea of endless *untrawþ*, nor does it provoke them to meditate on the condition of Satan and the damned. Gawain's particular strategy for giving meaning to his own experience is not successful because his views are doctrinally erroneous.

There is nothing inherently improper about the court's attempt to make the green girdle a sign for the renown of the Round Table; in the course of military history men have used sillier things as badges of honour. The difficulty with this meaning of the girdle, in this new context, comes in at the level of the communicating statement that each of the members of the court makes by adopting it and wearing it as sign. Its meaning is something like 'We too are only human, and we think we ought to be excused for our sins.' It is not in any way a penitential badge, or a reminder to do better; it is a claim to have done well enough. The contrast between such a sign and the pentangle, which calls on men to be worthy of participation in the endless bliss that is promised to the faithful, could not be more extreme.

The poem, of course, leaves us free to adopt the same attitude towards the court and their flaws and towards Gawain and his flaws, just as many modern readers feel that Augustine makes altogether too much fuss over a few pears. We have all sinned, and stories like this show that great men sin too; we might just as well relax, since we are just as deserving of being excused as Gawain and Arthur's court. It seems to me, however, that the *Gawain* poet expects us to see through this attitude as well as we see through Gawain's belief that he is perpetually flawed. When we examine the court's attempt at self-excuse, we may perhaps find it more subtle and more genteel than Gawain's anti-feminist tirade, but the attempt is basically the same. Instead of properly confessing their faults and proceeding on the path to redemption, all the participants in the narrative fall back into valuing earthly concerns more than God, and are 'running backwards.'

This is a depressing thought only for those who expect humans to be endlessly perfect by their own efforts. Such people, reading *Sir Gawain and the Green Knight* in this way, might well fall into a kind of despair. If not even the truest knight of the Round Table can maintain his truth, what hope is there for ordinary mortals? But both aspects of this attitude are indications of unorthodox beliefs about the effects of sin on our relationship to God. Excessive honour for human beings, on the ground that man was created in God's image, is an indication of a deviation from orthodox distinctions between God and man, especially God and fallen man. From an orthodox point of view, honour for Gawain as a perfect being is idolatrous and dangerous to his spiritual health since it tends to cause pride. Although man was created in God's image, he marred that image in the sin of Adam, so that no living human being could be thought to deserve the kind of honour that is due only to God. Even the man in a state of grace has attained only a conditional perfection, one that can easily be lost. Conversely, no living person in a state of sin, whether Gawain or a member of the court or the ordinary member of the audience, should be considered irredeemably lost. Those who hear the story of Gawain, or of Peter, or of Mary Magdalene, or of David, should realize that contrition, confession, and satisfaction can lead to salvation. Such a reading of the poem provokes the reader to move towards the enjoyment of God for God's own sake and to the enjoyment of one's self and one's neighbour for the sake of God.[41]

Notes

INTRODUCTION

1 Randall 'Was the Green Knight a Fiend?'; Highfield 'The Green Squire'; Long 'Was the Green Knight Really Merlin?'
2 Krappe 'Who *Was* the Green Knight?'; Braddy 'Sir Gawain and Ralph Holmes the Green Knight'; Schnyder *Sir Gawain and the Green Knight*
3 *Glossa Ordinaria*, PL 113, col 105B
4 This and all other unattributed translations are my own.
5 *Glossa Ordinaria*, PL 113, col 131A
6 *Allegoriae in Vetus Testamentum* col 647B
7 *Secreta Secretorum* 115
8 Ibid 230
9 Bloomfield *Essays and Explorations* 88
10 Augustine *De Doctrina Christiana* III, xxv–xxvii (36–8)
11 Augustine *On Christian Doctrine* 100–2
12 *De Doctrina* I, ii (2)
13 *On Christian Doctrine* 8
14 *De Doctrina* I, ii (2)
15 *On Christian Doctrine* 8–9
16 Peter Lombard *Sententiarum Libri Quatuor* I, I, cols 521–3
17 Sources for the study of sign theory in the fourteenth century fall into three categories. The works most widely known today are the *Peri Hermeneias* of Aristotle and Augustine's *De Doctrina*, both of which were in universal use. Secondly, we have the writings of the so-called terminist logicians, who supplemented the study of Aristotle with various tracts on the logic of terms. These tracts explored in minute detail the changes of meaning that occur when individual vocabulary items are used in larger propositions. Their ideas, which came to be the basis for all elementary instruction in logic in the thirteenth and four-teenth centuries, are most accessible in the tracts of William of Sherwood (ca 1200–70), Lambert of Auxerre (fl 1250), and Peter of Spain (ca 1205–

77). Peter's *Tractatus* are preserved in over three hundred manuscripts and two hundred printed editions, and it is reported by Jean Gerson (in *De Examinatione Doctrinarum*, in *Oeuvres complètes* 475) that they were given to schoolboys for memorization even before they were capable of understanding their contents. For certain points these works may be supplemented from the commentaries on the *Peri Hermeneias* by Ammonius, available in a thirteenth-century translation by Guillaume de Moerbeke, and by Aquinas. Finally, there are the works of the logicians of the fourteenth century, principally Ockham, which present notable advances and refinements in the field but principally in areas that are beyond the 'common knowledge' limits of my approach.

18 For a discussion of this point, see Maurer 'William of Ockham on Language and Reality' 795–802.
19 *De Doctrina* II, i (1)
20 *On Christian Doctrine* 34
21 *De Doctrina* I, vi (6)
22 *On Christian Doctrine* 10–11
23 Spade 'Epistemological Implications of the Burley-Ockham Dispute' 214
24 de Rijk *Logica Modernorum* vol 2, pt 1, p 123
25 Ibid p 124
26 Ibid p 125, n 1
27 Augustine *De Magistro* VII, 19
28 Augustine *The Teacher* 29–30
29 *Dives and Pauper*, EETS 275, pp 200–3

CHAPTER ONE: PURE SIGNIFICATION

1 All quotations are taken from *Sir Gawain and the Green Knight* ed Tolkien and Gordon.
2 In *Aristotle's Categories and De Interpretatione* trans Ackrill
3 Peter of Spain *Tractatus* 1
4 Ibid 2
5 Lambert of Auxerre *Logica* 7
6 William of Sherwood 'Die Introductiones in logicam des Wilhelm von Shyreswood' 31
7 William of Sherwood *Introduction to Logic* 23
8 Aquinas *In Aristotelis Libros Peri Hermeneias et Posteriorum Analyticorum Expositio* 11
9 Ammonius *Commentaire sur le Peri Hermeneias d'Aristote* 59
10 *De Doctrina* II, xxiv (37)
11 *On Christian Doctrine* 60
12 Chaucer *Troilus and Criseyde* II, 22–8, in *Works*, ed Robinson
13 *De Doctrina* II, i (1)
14 'De facto videmus quod unus circulus de certa materia tantum significat,

sicut faciet haec propositio scripta in pariete tabernae, "In hoc cellario est vinum." Unde hoc posset concedi, "Iste circulus est verus," quia sic est sicut per eum denotatur' (Courtenay, ed, 'A Revised Text of Robert Holcot's Quodlibetal Dispute' 7); 'We in fact see that a barrel-hoop of a certain material signifies as much as well the sentence "There is wine in this cellar," written on the wall. Hence, "This barrel-hoop is true" could be conceded, since the case is as is signified by it' (*Peter of Ailly: Concepts and Insolubles* 137, n 614).

15 Rabelais *Gargantua* chap 9, in *Oeuvres complètes* 66
16 Lambert of Auxerre *Logica* 7–8
17 Ibid 8, and Isidore of Seville *Etymologiarum sive Originum Libri* xx xi, i, 4, and xvi, iii, 1
18 Aquinas *In Aristotelis Libros* 21
19 Ammonius *Commentaire* 73. The point rests on Greek puns which Moerbeke does not attempt to reproduce.
20 Eberhard of Bethune *Graecismus* 47
21 Thomas Bradwardine *Geometria Speculativa* fol ii
22 Iohannes Belethus *Summa de Ecclesiasticis Officiis*, cccm 41a, p 248
23 In establishing this general background context I have used sources that are the type of material the poet might have read, sources that were unavailable to him but sum up currents of thought otherwise known to have been part of his culture, and sources that represent the sort of thing we might expect his audience to have heard in sermons.
24 Quotations from *Pearl* and *Purity* are taken from *The Works of the Gawain-Poet* ed Moorman.
25 *Dives and Pauper*, eets 280, pp 60–1
26 *Mirk's Festial* 291
27 *Middle English Sermons from ms. Roy. 18 b. xxiii* 250
28 Boethius *De Arithmetica* col 1137b; see also Hopper *Medieval Number Symbolism* 124–5.
29 Euclid, *Thirteen Books* xii, prop 7
30 Oresme *Quaestiones super Geometriam Euclidis* 12
31 Ibid 84
32 Ibid 12
33 Ibid 84
34 Bartholomaeus Anglicus *De Genuinis Rerum Coelestium, Terrestrium et Inferarum Proprietatibus Libri* xviii 12
35 *On the Properties of Things: John Trevisa's Translation of Bartholomaeus Anglicus De Proprietatibus Rerum* 53
36 Curtius *European Literature and the Latin Middle Ages* 353
37 Nicholas of Cusa *De Docta Ignorantia*, in *Nikolaus von Kues* 1: 234
38 Nicholas of Cusa *Nicolas Cusanus: Of Learned Ignorance* 28
39 *De Docta Ignorantia* 238–40
40 *Of Learned Ignorance* 32–3

41 *De Docta Ignorantia* 234
42 *Of Learned Ignorance* 28–9
43 Bartholomaeus Anglicus *De Proprietatibus Rerum* 12
44 *On the Properties of Things* 52–3
45 *De Docta Ignorantia* 260
46 *Of Learned Ignorance* 43
47 See Bradwardine *De Causa Dei* (1618), *Thomas of Bradwardine, His Tractatus de Proportionibus,* and *Geometria Speculativa,* and Murdoch 'Thomas Bradwardine' 395.
48 Sergescu *Le Développement de l'idée de l'infini mathématique au XIVᵉ siècle* 7
49 *De Docta Ignorantia* 260
50 *Of Learned Ignorance* 43
51 *De Docta Ignorantia* 232
52 *Of Learned Ignorance* 27–8
53 Anselm *Monologion* cxviii, in *Opera Omnia* 1: 32
54 Anselm *Monologion* 28–9
55 This and all other Latin biblical quotations are taken from *Biblia Sacra.*
56 This and the two following quotations from the Middle English Bible are taken from the Wycliffite version in *The English Hexapla.* Subsequent English versions are taken from the Douai-Rheims translation, as the closest approximation of the sense of the Vulgate.
57 Pecock *The Donet* 85
58 *Dives and Pauper,* EETS 275, pp 154, 232, 233, 234
59 Richard Lavynham *A Litil Tretys on the Seven Deadly Sins* 8
60 *Middle English Sermons* 45
61 Burrow *A Reading of Sir Gawain and the Green Knight* 187ff

CHAPTER TWO: THE USES OF A SIGN

1 Peter of Spain *Tractatus* 99
2 Dennys *The Heraldic Imagination* 42–3
3 *Dives and Pauper,* EETS 280, p 281
4 *The Sege off Melayne* 1465–73, 1475–6
5 *Sir Perceval of Gales* 1453–60, 1501–4
6 Franklyn *Shield and Crest* 4
7 *Tretis on Armes,* in *Medieval Heraldry: Some Fourteenth Century Heraldic Works* 213–14, 214
8 Dennys *Heraldic Imagination* 70
9 Evans 'Gawain's New Pentangle' 92–4
10 Ockham *Summa Logicae Pars Prima* 41
11 *Ockham's Theory of Terms: Part I of the Summa Logicae* 75–6
12 Bonet *The Tree of Battles* 203–4

13 Bartolo de Sassoferrato *De Insigniis et Armis*, in *Medieval Heraldry* 230–1
14 Brault *Early Blazon* 23
15 Neubecker *Heraldry: Sources, Symbols and Meaning* 37
16 Ibid 62
17 Franklyn *Shield and Crest* 259
18 *Medieval England* 363
19 Franklyn *Shield and Crest* 255
20 *Medieval England* 363
21 Magister Johannes de Bado Aureo *Tractatus de Armis*, in *Medieval Heraldry* 115, 116, 121; 120
22 Franklyn *Shield and Crest* 459
23 *De Doctrina* I, v (5)
24 *On Christian Doctrine* 10
25 Langland *Piers Plowman: The B Version* Passus XVI, 180–90
26 Dennys *Heraldic Imagination* 96
27 *Middle English Sermons* 38
28 Anderson *The Book of Psalms* 2: 592; Anderson's paraphrase of verse 6
29 Augustine *Enarrationes in Psalmos*, PL 37, col 1050
30 Adapted from *Saint Augustin: Expositions on the Book of Psalms* 396–7
31 *The St. Alban's Psalter (Albani Psalter)* 234–5; plate 65d.
32 [Rolle] *The Pricke of Conscience* 2048–65
33 Ibid 8283–96
34 Aristotle *On Sophistical Refutations* 27
35 Lambert *Logica* 184
36 *Summa Sophisticorum Elencorum*, in de Rijk *Logica Modernorum* I: 373
37 Stacey *Defamiliarization in Language and Literature* 163
38 *Carmina Burana* I: 38
39 Augustine *Enarrationes in Psalmos*, PL 37, col 1050
40 Adapted from *Saint Augustin: Expositions* 396–7
41 *The Cloud of Unknowing and the Book of Privy Counselling* 120
42 *Dan Michel's Ayenbite of Inwyt* 101
43 *Conciliorum Oecumenicorum Decreta* 232
44 Aquinas *Commentum in Matthaeum*, in *Sancti Thomae Aquinatis Opera Omnia* 66
45 *Medieval England* 362
46 Burke *Encyclopedia of Heraldry* entries 'Cross' and 'Christie'
47 Dennys *Heraldic Imagination* 97
48 Ibid
49 Riehle *The Middle English Mystics* 32
50 *Legends of the Holy Rood: Symbols of the Passion and Cross-Poems* 65–72, 97–100, 115–20
51 *De Docta Ignorantia* 270ff

52 Gregory *Epistola ad Serenum*; John of Damascus *Exposition of the Orthodox Faith* 88
53 *Dives and Pauper*, EETS 275, p 82
54 Netter *Doctrinale Antiquitatum Fidei Catholicae Ecclesiae* vol 3, col 921
55 Neubecker *Heraldry* 222
56 *Rolls of Arms: Henry III; The Matthew Paris Shields, c. 1244–59* 61; Neubecker *Heraldry* 222; Franklyn *Shield and Crest* 459; Dennys *Heraldic Imagination* 48
57 Holkott *Supra Libros Sapientiae* c iii, lectio xxxv. This passage is discussed also by I. Gollancz *Sir Gawain and the Green Knight*, EETS 210, *not. ad loc.*
58 Brinton *The Sermons of Thomas Brinton, Bishop of Rochester (1373–1389)* 266
59 *Middle English Sermons* 325–6
60 *Dives and Pauper*, EETS 280, p 309

CHAPTER THREE: FAITH AND TRUTH

1 *Cloud* 120, *Conciliorum Oecumenicorum Decreta* 232
2 *Middle English Sermons* 248
3 Ockham *Summa Logicae* 41–2
4 *Ockham's Theory of Terms* 76
5 Peter of Spain *Tractatus* 101
6 Anselm *Opera Omnia* 199
7 Anselm *Philosophical Fragments, De Grammatico, On Truth, etc* 106
8 *Gatryge's Sermon*, in *Religious Pieces in Prose and Verse* 10
9 *St. Edmund's Mirror*, in *Religious Pieces* 38
10 Rolle *English Prose Treatises of Richard Rolle de Hampole* 35–6
11 *Cursor Mundi: A Northumbrian Poem of the XIVth Century* 14072–3
12 *Pater Noster* 240–3, 255–8, in *Old English Homilies and Homiletic Treatises*
13 Langland *Piers Plowman* I, 12–16, 85–91
14 Murtaugh *Piers Plowman and the Image of God* 6. See also Harbert 'Truth, Love and Grace in the B-Text of *Piers Plowman*,' in Boitani and Torti *Literature in Fourteenth-Century England* 35.
15 *Cloud* 120
16 *The Book of Privy Counselling*, in *Cloud* 136
17 *Dives and Pauper*, EETS 280, pp 28–9, 31
18 Chaucer *Parson's Tale* 338–49, referring to I John 1:8
19 *Dives and Pauper*, EETS 275, p 94
20 *English Metrical Homilies from Manuscripts of the Fourteenth Century* 20
21 *Promptorium Parvulorum* 371

22 Radulphus Ardens, *Homiliae in Epistolas et Evangelia Dominicalia* col
   1759
23 '*Nescitis*, etc. Ostendit quanta sit utilitas legis nostrae, in qua non uni
   sed omnibus promissa est palma'; 'He shows how great is the utility
   of our law, in which the prize is promised not to one but to all' (*Glossa
   Ordinaria, PL* 114, col 534).
24 *Mirk's Festial: A Collection of Homilies by Johannes Mirkus (John Mirk)*
   65
25 Wyclif *Select English Works* 2:257–8
26 Iohannes Belethus *Summa, CCCM* 41a, pp 140–1
27 Wyclif *Select English Works* 2:258–9
28 Augustine *De Trinitate, CCSL* 50, IV, xviii (24), quoting Plato *Timaeus*
   29c and John 17:3
29 Augustine *The Trinity* 160–1

CHAPTER FOUR: THE GIRDLE AND THE WOUND

 1 The complexity of the various possibilities for treating the green girdle
   as a sign for a particular referent has come to be recognized in recent
   years as a part of the poet's choice to make 'interpretation' one of the
   themes of his poem. See, for example, Ralph Hanna, 'Unlocking What's
   Locked: Gawain's Green Girdle.' Hanna's concern with the text itself
   is refreshing, but his reliance on new critical methods prevents him
   from seeing some of the historically based distinctions between apparently similar impositions of meanings. Similarly, R.A. Shoaf, in *The
   Poem as Green Girdle* 67ff, makes some interesting suggestions, but his
   unquestioning acceptance of Burrow's ahistorical distinctions concerning
   natural and *ad placitum* signification, and his rapid shift from medieval
   sign-theory to modern semiotic methods, lead to a view of the material
   rather different from my own.
 2 *Dives and Pauper, EETS* 275, p 154; 280, p 103
 3 *Middle English Sermons* 111
 4 Anselm *Meditatio VI, PL* 158, col 738c
 5 *Jacob's Well* 67
 6 *English Metrical Homilies* 15–16
 7 *Jacob's Well* 112, 113
 8 Peter Lombard *Sententiarum Libri Quatuor* col 877
 9 Chaucer *Parson's Tale* 106–7
10 For a general discussion see Entralgo *Mind and Body* 71ff.
11 *De Doctrina* I, xiv (13)
12 *On Christian Doctrine* 14–15
13 *Middle English Sermons* 307
14 *Conciliorum Oecumenicorum Decreta* 245
15 *Jacob's Well* 178

16 *Sir Gawain and the Green Knight* ed Gollancz *not. ad loc.*
17 See Moorman's note, in *The Works of the Gawain Poet* 442.
18 *The Pricke of Conscience* 8297–316, 8317–23, 8352–62
19 Langland *Piers Plowman* XIV, 95–7
20 *Mirk's Festial* 2

CHAPTER FIVE: GAWAIN AS EXEMPLARY INDIVIDUAL

1 Kolve *The Play Called Corpus Christi* 102
2 *Jacob's Well* 175–6
3 *The Book of Vices and Virtues* 174–5
4 *Speculum Sacerdotale* 65
5 *Middle English Sermons* 276
6 [Augustine] *Sermo* CCLVI: *Admonitio per quam ostenditur* col 2219
7 *Twenty-Six Political and Other Poems* 34
8 *The Book of Vices and Virtues* 175
9 *Dan Michel's Ayenbite of Inwit* 173
10 'A Good Stirring Heavenward' 169–76, in *Twenty-Six Political and Other Poems* 45
11 'First Sunday in Lent,' in *Old English Homilies* 29
12 Ibid 28
13 'Of Women cometh this Worldes Weal' 25–36, in *The Minor Poems of the Vernon MS* 705
14 There is a considerable amount of discussion of this speech in the critical literature, most of it centred on its anti-feminism. See, for example, David Mills 'The Rhetorical Function of Gawain's Antifeminism?' Mary Dove 'Gawain and the *Blasme des Femmes* Tradition,' and P.J. Lucas 'Gawain's Anti-Feminism.' Even John Burrow, who notes that '*Sir Gawain* is concerned with women's wiles no more than it is with chastity' (*Reading* 148), sidesteps the question of the impropriety of Gawain's attempt to be excused for his sin.
15 'Proverbs of Prophets, Poets and Saints' 35–8, in *The Minor Poems of the Vernon MS* 524
16 *Jacob's Well* 171, 182
17 Ibid 180–1
18 *The Book of Vices and Virtues* 177
19 *Speculum Sacerdotale* 65
20 *Dives and Pauper*, EETS 280, pp 80–7
21 Rolle *English Prose Treatises* 10
22 Wyclif *De Mandatis Divinis*, in *Johannis Wyclif: Tractatus de Mandatis Divinis and Tractatus de Statu Innocencie* 156, 157
23 Wyclif *Iohannes Wyclif: De Eucharista* 318
24 See Gower *Vox Clamantis* II, 551, in *Complete Works*; and Clement of

Alexandria *Exhortation to the Heathen*, chap 4. See also Minnis *Chaucer and Pagan Antiquity* 38ff.

25 Quoted in Dymmok, *Liber contra xii Errores et Hereses Lollardorum* 180
26 *An Apology for Lollard Doctrine Attributed to Wicliffe* 85
27 Pecock *The Repressor of Over Much Blaming of the Clergy* 1:193
28 See *Heresy Trials in the Diocese of Norwich, 1428–31* 71, 78, 81, 87, 98, 101, 142, 154; *Selections from English Wycliffite Writings* 36, 84; Foxe *The Acts and Monuments* 223, 265, 334.
29 Pelikan *The Spirit of Eastern Christendom (600–1700)* 91–145
30 Netter *Doctrinale* vol 3, col 929
31 Pecock *Repressor* 220–1, 221
32 Dymmok *Liber contra xii Errores* 188
33 *Selections from English Wycliffite Writings* 179–80
34 Map *De Nugis Curialium* 1–2
35 Map *De Nugis Curialium (Courtiers' Trifles)* 1–2
36 Cassiodorus *Expositiones in Psalmos*, CCSL 98, p 452
37 Augustine *Enarrationes in Psalmos*, PL 36, cols 586–7
38 Augustine *Saint Augustin: Expositions* 190
39 Gregory *Moralia in Job*, PL 76, col 687, and *Glossa Ordinaria*, PL 113, col 572
40 Gregory *Morals of the Book of Job* 3: 578–9. See also Minnis *Medieval Theory of Authorship* 103ff.
41 *De Doctrina* iii, x (16); *On Christian Doctrine* 88

Bibliography

PRIMARY SOURCES

Allegoriae in Vetus Testamentum. PL 175, cols 635–750

Ammonius. *Commentaire sur le Peri Hermeneias d'Aristote.* Trans Guillaume de Moerbeke, ed G. Verbecke. Louvain: Publications Universitaires de Louvain 1961

Anselm of Canterbury. *Meditatio VI.* PL 158, cols 736–40

– *Monologion, Proslogion, Debate with Gaunilo and a Meditation on Human Redemption.* Trans Jasper Hopkins and Herbert Richardson. Toronto: Edwin Mellen Press 1974

– *Opera Omnia.* Ed F.S. Schmitt. Secovii 1938

– *Philosophical Fragments, De Grammatico, On Truth, etc.* Trans Jasper Hopkins and Herbert Richardson. Toronto: Edwin Mellen Press 1976

An Apology for Lollard Doctrines Attributed to Wicliffe. Ed J.H. Todd. Camden Society 1842; repr New York: AMS Press 1968

Aquinas, Thomas. *Commentum in Mattheum.* In *Sancti Thomae Aquinatis Opera Omnia.* New York: Musurgia 1949

– *In Aristotelis Libros Peri Hermeneias et Posteriorum Analyticorum Expositio.* Ed R.M. Spiazzi. Torino: Marietti 1955

Aristotle. *Aristotle's Categories and De Interpretatione.* Trans J.L. Ackrill. Oxford: Clarendon Press 1963

– *On Sophistical Refutations.* Trans E.S. Forster. London: William Heinemann 1955

Augustine. *De Doctrina Christiana.* Ed Joseph Martin. CCSL 32

De Magistro. Ed K.-D. Daur. CCSL 29

De Trinitate. Ed W.J. Mountain. CCSL 50 50a

– *Enarrationes in Psalmos.* PL 36, 37

– *Esposizioni Sui Salmi.* Ed R. Minuti. Rome: Citta Nuova Editrice 1967

– *On Christian Doctrine.* Trans D.W. Robertson, Jr. Indianapolis: Bobbs Merrill 1958

– *Saint Augustin: Expositions on the Book of Psalms*. Trans P. Schaff.
  Grand Rapids: Eerdmans 1956
– *The Teacher*. Trans R.P. Russell. Vol 59 of *The Fathers of the Church*.
  Washington: Catholic University of America 1968
– *The Trinity*. Trans Stephen McKenna. Washington: Catholic University of
  America Press 1963
[Augustine] *Sermo* CCLVI: *Admonitio per quam ostenditur* ... PL 39, cols
  2219–23
Bacon, Roger. *The Opus Majus of Roger Bacon*. Trans Robert Belle Burke.
  New York: Russell and Russell 1962
Bartholomaeus Anglicus. *De Genuinis Rerum Colestium, Terrestrium, et
  Inferarum Proprietatibus Libri* XVIII. Ed Georgius Bartholdus Pontanus.
  Frankfurt: Wolfgang Richter 1601; repr Frankfurt: Minerva 1964
Biblia Sacra. Ed Alberto Colunga and Laurentio Turrado. Madrid: Biblioteca
  de Autores Cristianos 1965
Boethius, Anicius Manlius Severinus. *De Arithmetica*. PL 63, cols 1079–
  1168
Bonet, Honoré. *The Tree of Battles*. Trans G.W. Coopland. Liverpool:
  University Press 1949
The Book of Vices and Virtues. Ed W.N. Francis. EETS 217
Bradwardine, Thomas. *De Causa Dei contra Pelagianos*. London: Henry
  Saville 1618; repr Frankfurt: Minerva 1964
– *Geometria Speculativa*. Paris: Marchant 1495
– *Thomas of Bradwardine, His Tractatus de Proportionibus*. Ed H. Lamar
  Crosby. Madison: University of Wisconsin Press 1955
Brinton, Thomas. *The Sermons of Thomas Brinton, Bishop of Rochester
  (1373–1389)*. Ed Sr M.A. Devlin London: Office Of the Royal Historical
  Society 1954
Carmina Burana. Ed A. Hilka and O. Schumann. Heidelberg: Carl Winter
  1978
Cassiodorus. *Expositiones in Psalmos*. Ed M. Adriaen. CCSL 97, 98
Catholicon Anglicum: An English-Latin Wordbook. Ed Sidney J.H. Herrtage.
  EETS OS 75
Chaucer, Geoffrey. *The Complete Works of Geoffrey Chaucer*. Ed
  F.N. Robinson. 2nd edn. Boston: Houghton Mifflin 1957
Clement of Alexandria. *Exhortation to the Heathen*. Trans A. Roberts and
  J. Donaldson. In *Ante-Nicene Christian Library*, vol 4. Edinburgh: Clark
  1867
The Cloud of Unknowing and the Book of Privy Counselling. Ed Phyllis
  Hodgson. EETS 218.
Conciliorum Oecumenicorum Decreta. Ed Joseph Alberigo et al. Bologna:
  Istituto per le scienze religiose 1973
Courtenay, William J., ed. 'A Revised Text of Robert Holcot's Quodlibetal
  Dispute on Whether God Is Able to Know More than He Knows.' *Archiv
  für Geschichte der Philosophie* 53 (1971): 94–119

Cursor Mundi: A Northumbrian Poem of the xivth Century. Ed R. Morris. EETS os 62

Dan Michel's Ayenbite of Inwyt. Ed R. Morris and P. Gradon. EETS os 23

Dean, Ruth J. 'An Early Treatise on Heraldry in Anglo-Norman.' In *Romance Studies in Memory of Edward Billings Ham.* Ed Urban Tigner Holmes. Hayward: California State College Publications 1967

de Rijk, L.M. *Logica Modernorum: A Contribution to the History of Early Terminist Logic.* Assen: Van Gorcum 1962

Dives and Pauper. Ed P.H. Barnum. EETS 275, 280

Dymmok, Roger. *Liber contra xii Errores et Hereses Lollardorum* Ed H.S. Cronin. London: Kegan Paul, Trench, Teubner, nd

Eberhard of Bethune. *Graecismus.* Ed J. Wrobel. Bratislava: Koebner 1887

The English Hexapla. London: Samuel Bagster and Sons 1841

English Metrical Homilies from Manuscripts of the Fourteenth Century. Ed John Small. Edinburgh: William Patterson 1862

Euclid. *The Thirteen Books of Euclid's Elements.* Trans T.L. Heath. New York: Dover 1956

Foxe, John. *The Acts and Monuments of John Foxe.* Ed S.R. Cattley. London: Seeley and Burnside 1837

Gerson, Jean. *Oeuvres complètes.* Paris: Desclée 1973

Glossa Ordinaria. See Strabo

Gollancz. See *Sir Gawain*

Gower, John. *The Complete Works of John Gower* vol. 4 *The Latin Works.* Ed G.C. Macaulay. Oxford: Clarendon Press 1902

Gregory. *Epistola ad Serenum.* PL 77, cols 1128–30

– *Moralia in Job.* PL 75, 76

– *Morals on the Book of Job.* 3 vols. Oxford: John Henry Parker 1845–7

Henry of Lancaster. *Le Livre de seyntz medicines.* Ed E.J. Arnould. Oxford: Anglo-Norman Text Society 1940

Heresy Trials in the Diocese of Norwich, 1428–31. Ed N.P. Tanner. Camden Fourth Series 20. London: Offices of the Royal Historical Society 1977

Holkott, Robert. *Supra Libros Sapienitiae.* Hagenau 1494; repr Frankfurt: Minerva 1974

Iohannes Belethus. *Summa de Ecclesiasticis Officiis.* Ed H. Douteil. CCCM, 41, 41a

Isidore of Seville. *Etymologiarum sive Originum Libri xx.* Ed W.M. Lindsay. Oxford: Clarendon Press 1911

Jacob's Well: An Englisht Treatise of the Cleansing of Man's Conscience. Ed Arthur Brandeis. EETS os 115

John of Damascus. *Exposition of the Orthodox Faith.* Trans S.D.F. Salmon. A Select Series of Nicene and Post-Nicene Fathers, 2nd ser, vol 19. New York: Charles Scribner's Sons 1899

Lambert of Auxerre. *Logica (Summa Lamberti).* Ed Franco Alessio. Firenze: La Nuova Italia editrice 1971

Langland, William. *Piers Plowman: The B Version*. Ed George Kane and
E. Talbot Donaldson. London: Athlone Press 1975

Lavynham, Richard. *A Litil Tretys of the Seven Deadly Sins*. Ed J. Van
Zutphen. Rome: Institutum Carmelitanum 1956

Legends of the Holy Rood: Symbols of the Passion and Cross-Poems. Ed
R. Morris. *EETS* OS 46

Mannyng, Robert. *Handlyng Synne*. Ed Idelle Sullens. Binghamton: Medieval
and Renaissance Texts & Studies 1983

Map, Walter. *De Nugis Curialium*. Ed M.R. James. Anecdota Oxoniensa,
Mediaeval and Modern Series, 1914

– *De Nugis Curialium (Courtiers' Trifles)*. Trans Frederick Tupper and
Marburg Ogle. London: Chatto and Windus 1929

Medieval Handbooks of Penance. Ed John T. McNeill and Helen M. Garner.
Columbia University Records of Civilization, no 29. New York: Columbia University Press 1938

Medieval Heraldry: Some Fourteenth-Century Heraldic Works. Ed Evan
John Jones. Cardiff: William Lewis 1943

Middle English Sermons from MS. Roy. 18 B. xxiii. Ed Woodburn O. Ross.
EETS 209

The Minor Poems of the Vernon MS. Ed F.J. Furnivall. Pt 2. *EETS* OS 117

Mirk's Festial: A Collection of Homilies by Johannes Mirkus (John Mirk).
Ed T. Erbe. *EETS* es 96

Moorman. See *Works of the Gawain-Poet*

Mullaly, Joseph Patrick.*The Summule Logicales of Peter of Spain*. Notre
Dame Publications in Medieval Studies 8. Notre Dame: University of
Notre Dame Press 1945

Netter, Thomas. *Doctrinale Antiquitatum Fidei Catholicae Ecclesiae*. Ed
G. Blanciotti. Venice 1757–9; repr 3 vols, Farnborough: Gregg Press 1967

Nicholas of Cusa. *Nicolas Cusanus: Of Learned Ignorance*. Trans G. Heron.
London: Routledge and Kegan Paul 1954

– *Nikolaus von Kues: Philosophisch-theologische Schrifte*. Ed Leo Gabriel.
2 vols. Wien: Verlag Herder 1964

Ockham, William. *Ockham's Theory of Terms: Part I of the Summa Logicae*.
Trans M.J. Loux. Notre Dame: Notre Dame University Press 1974

– *Summa Logicae Pars Prima*. Ed Philotheus Boehner. St Bonaventure:
Franciscan Institute 1957

Old English Homilies and Homiletic Treatises. Ed R. Morris. *EETS* OS 29

*On the Properties of Things: John Trevisa's Translation of Bartholomaeus
Anglicus De Proprietatibus Rerum*. Oxford: Clarendon Press 1975

Oresme, Nicholas. *Quaestiones super Geometriam Euclidis*. Ed H.L.L.
Busard. Leiden: E.J. Brill 1961

Pecock, Reginald. *The Donet*. Ed E.V. Hitchcock. *EETS* OS 156

– *The Repressor of Over Much Blaming of the Clergy*. Ed Churchill
Babington. Rolls Series no 19. London: Longman, Green, Longman and
Roberts 1860

Peter Lombard. *Sententiarum Libri Quatuor*. PL 192.

Peter of Ailly: Concepts and Insolubles. Trans Paul Vincent Spade. Dordrecht: Reidel 1980

Peter of Spain. *Tractatus called afterwards Summule Logicales*. Ed L.M. de Rijk. Assen: Van Gorcum 1972

Porphyry the Phoenician. *Isagoge*. Trans Edward W. Warren. Toronto: Pontifical Institute of Mediaeval Studies 1975

The Promptorium Parvulorum: The First English-Latin Dictionary. Ed A.L. Mayhew. EETS es 102

Rabelais, François. *Oeuvres complètes*. Ed Guy Demerson. Paris: Editions du Seuil 1973

Radulphus Ardens. *Homiliae in Epistolas et Evangelia Dominicalia*. PL 155, cols 1665–2118

Religious Pieces in Prose and Verse. Ed G.G. Perry. EETS os 26

Robert of Flamborough. *Liber Poenitentialis*. Ed J.J.F. Firth. Toronto: Pontifical Institute of Mediaeval Studies 1971

Rolle, Richard. *English Prose Treatises of Richard Rolle de Hampole*. Ed G.G. Perry. EETS os 20

[Rolle, Richard] *The Pricke of Conscience*. Ed R. Morris. Berlin: Asher 1863

Rolls of Arms: Henry III; The Matthew Paris Shields, c. 1244–59. Ed T.D. Tremlett. London: University Press 1967

Secreta Secretorum. Ed R. Steele. EETS es 74

The Sege off Melayne. Ed S.J. Herrtage. EETS es 35

Selections from English Wycliffite Writings. Ed Anne Hudson. Cambridge: Cambridge University Press 1978

Sir Gawain and the Green Knight. Ed Israel Gollancz. EETS 210

Sir Gawain and the Green Knight. Ed J.R.R. Tolkien and E.V. Gordon. 2nd edn rev Norman Davis. Oxford: Clarendon Press 1967

Sir Perceval of Gales. Ed J. Campion and F. Holthausen. Heidelberg: Carl Winter 1913

Speculum Sacerdotale. Ed Edward H. Weatherly. EETS 200

The St. Alban's Psalter (Albani Psalter). Ed Otto Pacht and C.R. Dodwell. London: Warburg Institute 1960

Strabo, Walafrid. *Glossa Ordinaria*. PL 113, 114

Twenty-Six Political and Other Poems (Excluding 'Petty Job') from the Oxford MSS Digby 102 and Douce 322. Ed J. Kail. EETS os 124

William of Sherwood. 'Die Introductiones in Logicam des Wilhelm von Shyreswood († nach 1267).' In *Sitzungsberichte der Bayerischen Akademie der Wissenschaften*. Ed Martin Grabmann. Philosophisch-historische Klasse, Jahrgang 1937, Heft 10

– *Introduction to Logic*. Trans Norman Kretzman. Minneapolis: University of Minnesota Press 1966

The Works of the Gawain-Poet. Ed Charles Moorman. Jackson: University of Mississippi Press 1977

Wright, Thomas. *A Volume of Vocabularies*. London 1857

Wyclif, John. *Iohannes Wyclif: De Eucharista*. Ed Iohann Loserth. London: Trubner 1892
– *Johannis Wyclif: Tractatus de Mandatis Divinis and Tractatus de Statu Innocencie*. Ed J. Loserth and F.D. Matthew. London: Kegan Paul 1922
– *Select English Works of John Wyclif*. Ed Thomas Arnold. Oxford: Clarendon Press 1871

SECONDARY SOURCES

Ackerman, Robert W. 'Gawain's Shield: Penitential Doctrine in *Gawain and the Green Knight*.' *Anglia* 76 (1956): 254–65
Anderson, A.A. *The Book of Psalms*. London: Oliphant's 1972
Arthur, Ross G. 'A Head for a Head: A Testamental Template for *Sir Gawain and the Green Knight* and *The Wife of Bath's Tale*.' *Florilegium* 6 (1984): 178–94
Baldwin, Thomas W. *William Shakspere's Small Latine & Less Greeke*. 2 vols. Urbana: University of Illinois Press 1944
Barnard, Leslie W. *The Greco-Roman and Oriental Background of the Iconolclastic Controversy*. Leiden: Brill 1974
Benson, Larry D. *Art and Tradition in Sir Gawain and the Green Knight*. New Brunswick, NJ: Rutgers University Press 1965
Bloomfield, Morton W. *Essays and Explorations*. Cambridge, Mass: Harvard University Press 1970
Bochenski, Innocentius M. *A History of Formal Logic*. Trans Ivo Thomas. Notre Dame: University of Notre Dame Press 1961
Boehner, Philotheus. *Medieval Logic: An Outline of Its Development from 1250 to c. 1400*. Manchester: Manchester University Press 1952
Boitani, Piero, and Anna Torti, eds. *Literature in Fourteenth-Century England*. Cambridge: D.S. Brewer 1983
Braddy, Haldeen. 'Sir Gawain and Ralph Holmes the Green Knight.' *Modern Language Notes* 67 (1952): 240–2
Brault, Gerald J. *Early Blazon*. Oxford: Clarendon Press 1972
Bruten, Avril K. 'Gawain's Green Girdle as a "Sign." ' *Notes and Queries* ns 13 (Dec 1966): 452–4
Burke, John. *Encyclopaedia of Heraldry*. London nd
Burrow, J.A. ' "Cupiditas" in *Sir Gawain and the Green Knight*.' *Review of English Studies* ns 15 (1964): 56
– *A Reading of Sir Gawain and the Green Knight*. London: Routledge and Kegan Paul 1965
– *Ricardian Poetry: Chaucer, Gower, Langland, and the 'Gawain' Poet*. London: Routledge and Kegan Paul 1971
Champion, Larry S. 'Grace versus Merit in *Sir Gawain and the Green Knight*.' *Modern Language Quarterly* 28 (1967): 413–25

Clanchy, M.T. *From Memory to Written Record: England,* 1066–1307. Cambridge, Mass: Harvard University Press 1979

Colish, Marcia L. *The Mirror of Language: A Study in the Medieval Theory of Knowledge.* New Haven: Yale University Press 1968

Copleston, Frederick. *Ockham to the Speculative Mystics.* Pt 1 of *Late Medieval and Early Renaissance Philosophy.* Vol 3 of *A History of Philosophy.* Garden City: Image Books 1963

Curtius, E.R. *European Literature and the Latin Middle Ages.* Trans W.R. Trask. Princeton: Princeton University Press 1953

Davenport, W.A. *The Art of the Gawain Poet.* London: Athlone 1978

Dennys, Rodney. *The Heraldic Imagination.* London: Barrie and Jenkins 1975

Derrickson, Ann. 'The Pentangle: Guiding Star for the *Gawain*-Poet.' *Comitatus* 11 (1980): 10–19

Dove, Mary. 'Gawain and the *Blasme des Femmes* Tradition.' *Medium Aevum* 46 (1972): 20–6

Eagan, Joseph F. *The Import of Color Symbolism in Sir Gawain and the Green Knight.* St Louis University Studies, ser A, 1 (1949)

Eldredge, Laurence. 'Late Medieval Discussions of the Continuum and the Point of the Middle English *Patience.*' *Vivarium* 17 (1979): 90–115

Entralgo, Pedro L. *Mind and Body: Psychosomatic Pathology: A Short History of the Evolution of Medical Thought.* London: Harvill nd

Evans, W.O. 'Gawain's New Pentangle.' *Trivium* 3 (1968): 92–4

Finlayson, John. 'The Expectations of Romance in *Sir Gawain and the Green Knight.*' *Genre* 12 (1979): 1–24

Flew, R. Newton. *The Idea of Perfection in Christian Theology.* Oxford: Clarendon Press 1934; repr 1968

Foley, Michael M. 'Gawain's Two Confessions Reconsidered.' *Chaucer Review* 9 (1974): 73–9

Franklyn, Julian. *Shield and Crest: An Account of the Art and Science of Heraldry.* London: MacGibbon and Kee 1967

Friedman, Albert B., and Richard H. Osberg. 'Gawain's Girdle as Traditional Symbol.' *Journal of American Folklore* 90 (1977): 301–15

Gabriel, Astrik L. *Garlandia: Studies in the History of the Medieval University.* Notre Dame: Mediaeval Institute, University of Notre Dame, 1969

Gairdner, James. *Lollardy and the Reformation in England.* 4 vols. London: Macmillan 1908–13

Green, Richard Hamilton. 'Gawain's Shield and the Quest for Perfection.' In *Middle English Survey.* Ed Edward Vasta. Notre Dame: University of Notre Dame Press 1965, pp 71–92

Gross, Laila. 'Gawain's Acceptance of the Girdle.' *American Notes and Queries* 12 (1974): 154–5

Haines, Victor Y. 'When Gawain Sins?' *Revue de l'Université d'Ottawa* 46 (1976): 242–6

Hanna, Ralph. 'Unlocking What's Locked: Gawain's Green Girdle.' *Viator* 14 (1983): 289–302

Hendrix, Howard V. ' "To Luf Hom Wel, and Leve Hem Not": The Neglected Humor of Gawain's "Antifeminism." ' *Comitatus* 14 (1983): 39–48

Hieatt, A. Kent. '*Sir Gawain*: Pentangle, *Luf-Lace*, Numerical Structure.' *Papers on Language and Literature* 4 (1968): 339–59

Highfield, J.R.L. 'The Green Squire.' *Medium Ævum* 22 (1953): 18–23

Hills, David Farley. 'Gawain's Fault in *Sir Gawain and the Green Knight*.' *Review of English Studies* ns 14 (1963): 124–31

Hopper, V.F. *Medieval Number Symbolism*. New York: Columbia University Press 1938 repr Cooper Square 1969

Hunt, Tony. 'Gawain's Fault and the Moral Perspectives of *Sir Gawain and the Green Knight*.' *Trivium* 10 (1975): 1–18

Jackson, Isaac. 'Sir Gawain's Coat of Arms.' *Modern Language Review* 15 (1920): 77–9

Jacobs, Nicholas. 'Gawain's False Confession.' *English Studies* 51 (1970): 433–5

Jeffrey, David L., ed. *By Things Seen: Reference and Recognition in Medieval Thought*. Ottawa: University of Ottawa Press 1979

Johnson, Lynn Staley. *The Voice of the Gawain-Poet*. Madison: University of Wisconsin Press 1984

Jones, William R. 'Art and Christian Piety: Iconoclasm in Medieval Europe.' In *The Image and the Word: Confrontation in Judaism, Christianity, and Islam*. Ed Joseph Gutman. Missoula: Scholar's Press 1977, pp. 27–50

– 'Lollards and Images: The Defense of Religious Art in Later Medieval England.' *Journal of the History of Ideas* 34 (1979): 27–50

Kindrick, Robert L. 'Gawain's Ethics: Shame and Guilt in *Sir Gawain and the Green Knight*.' *Annuale Medievale* 20 (1981): 5–32

Kneale, William, and Martha Kneale. *The Development of Logic*. Oxford: Clarendon Press 1962

Knowles, David. *The English Mystical Tradition*. New York: Harper 1961

Knowlton, Sr Mary Arthur. *The Influence of Richard Rolle and of Julian of Norwich on the Middle English Lyrics*. The Hague: Mouton 1973

Kolve, V.A. *The Play Called Corpus Christi*. Stanford: Stanford University Press 1966

Kottler, Barnet, and Alan M. Markman. *A Concordance to Five Middle English Poems: Cleanness, St. Erkenwald, Sir Gawain and the Green Knight, Patience, Pearl*. Pittsburgh: University of Pittsburgh Press 1966

Krappe, A.H. 'Who Was the Green Knight?' *Speculum* 13 (1938): 206–15

Lass, Roger. ' "Man's Heaven": The Symbolism of Gawain's Shield.' *Mediaeval Studies* 28 (1966): 354–60

Leff, Gordon. *The Dissolution of the Medieval Outlook*. New York: New York University Press 1976

– *John Wyclif: The Path to Dissent*. London: Oxford University Press 1966

Lewis, C.S. 'The Anthropological Approach.' In *English and Medieval Studies Presented to J.R.R. Tolkien on the Occasion of His Seventieth*

Birthday. Ed Norman Davis and C.L. Wrenn. London: Allen and Unwin 1962, pp. 219–310

Long, Charles. 'Was the Green Knight Really Merlin?' *Interpretations* 7 (1975): 1–7

Loomis, Roger Sherman. 'More Celtic Elements in *Gawain and the Green Knight.*' *Journal of English and Germanic Philology* 42 (1943): 149–84

Lucas, P.J. 'Gawain's Anti-Feminism.' *Notes and Queries* ns 15 (1968): 324–5

Manning, Stephen. 'A Psychological Interpretation of *Sir Gawain and the Green Knight.*' *Criticism* 6 (1964): 165–77

Mathew, Gervase. *Byzantine Aesthetics*. London: John Murray 1963

Maurer, Armand. 'William of Ockham on Language and Reality.' *Miscellanea Mediaevalia* 13, no 2 (1981): 795–802

Medieval England. Ed Austin Lane Poole. Oxford: Clarendon Press 1958

Mills, David. 'The Rhetorical Function of Gawain's Antifeminism?' *Neuphilologische Mitteilungen* 71 (1970): 635–40

Minnis, A.J. *Chaucer and Pagan Antiquity*. Cambridge: D.S. Brewer 1982

– *Medieval Theory of Authorship*. London: Scolar Press 1984

Morgan, Gerald. 'The Significance of the Pentangle Symbolism in "Sir Gawain and the Green Knight." ' *Modern Language Review* 74 (1979): 769–90

– 'The Validity of Gawain's Confession in *Sir Gawain and the Green Knight.*' *Review of English Studies* 36 (1985): 1–18

Murdoch, John E. 'Thomas Bradwardine.' In *Dictionary of Scientific Biography*. Ed C.C. Gillispie. New York: Charles Scribner's Sons 1970

Murtaugh, Daniel Maher. *Piers Plowman and the Image of God*. Gainesville: University Presses of Florida 1978

Neaman, Judith. 'Sir Gawains Covenant: Troth and Timor Mortis.' *Philological Quarterly* 55 (1976): 30–42

Neubecker, Ottfried. *Heraldry: Sources, Symbols and Meaning*. New York: McGraw Hill 1976

Nolan, Barbara. *The Gothic Visionary Perspective*. Princeton: Princeton University Press 1977

Ong, Walter J. 'The Green Knight's Harts and Bucks.' *Modern Language Notes* 65 (1950): 536–9

Orme, Nicholas. *English Schools in the Middle Ages*. London: Methuen 1973

Paetow, Louis John. *The Arts Course at Medieval Universities with Special Reference to Grammar and Rhetoric*. Champaign: University of Illinois Press 1910

Passmore, John. *The Perfectibility of Man*. New York: Charles Scribner's Sons 1976

Pastoureau, Michel. *Traité d'héraldique*. Paris: Picard 1979

Pelikan, Jaroslav. *The Spirit of Eastern Christendom (600–1700)*. Vol 2 of *The Christian Tradition*. Chicago: University of Chicago Press 1974

Pine, L.G. *The Story of Heraldry*. Rutland, Vt: Charles E. Tuttle 1966

Randall, Dale B.J. 'Was the Green Knight a Fiend?' *Studies in Philology* 57
  (1960): 479–91
Riehle, Wolfgang. *The Middle English Mystics.* Trans Bernard Standring.
  London: Routledge and Kegan Paul 1981
Robertson, D.W., Jr. 'Why the Devil Wears Green.' *Modern Language Notes*
  69 (1954): 470–2
Schnyder, Hans. *Sir Gawain and the Green Knight: An Essay in Interpreta-*
  tion. Cooper Monographs on English and American Literature 6. Bern:
  Francke 1961
Sergescu, Pierre. *Le Développement de l'idée de l'infini mathématique au*
  XIVᵉ siècle. Paris: Université de Paris 1947
Shoaf, R.A. *The Poem as Green Girdle: Commercium in Sir Gawain and*
  the Green Knight. Gainesville: University Presses of Florida 1984
Spade, Paul Vincent. 'Epistemological Implications of the Burley-Ockham
  Dispute.' *Franciscan Studies* 75 (1977): 212–36
Speirs, John. *Medieval English Poetry: The Non-Chaucerian Tradition.*
  London: Faber and Faber 1957
Stacey, R.H. *Defamiliarization in Language and Literature.* Syracuse: Syra-
  cuse University Press 1977
Thorndike, Lynn. ''Elementary and Secondary Education in the Middle
  Ages.' *Speculum* 15 (1940): 400–8
Wagner, Anthony R. *A Catalogue of English Medieval Rolls of Arms.*
  Oxford: Society of Antiquaries 1950
– *Heralds and Heraldry in the Middle Ages.* 2nd edn. London: Oxford
  University Press 1956
Weishepl, J.A. 'Curriculum of the Faculty of Arts at Oxford in the Early
  Fourteenth Century.' *Mediaeval Studies* 28 (1966): 151–75
White, Robert B., Jr. 'A Note on the Green Knight's Red Eyes (*Gawain and*
  the Green Knight, 304).' *English Language Notes* 2 (1965): 150–2

Index

Medieval Sign Theory and
Sir Gawain and the Green Knight

ROSS G. ARTHUR

The formal theory of signs taught in four-teenth-century schools and its analytic techniques were familiar to all educated Englishmen of the period, whether directly from the standard texts or indirectly through their manifestations in sermons, popularizing poetry, and discussions of heraldic practice. In this book Ross Arthur seeks to understand *Sir Gawain and the Green Knight* in terms of the poet's creative use of that theory.

Its relevance to *Sir Gawain* is clearest in connection with the poem's most explicitly symbolic objects: the pentangle, the green girdle, and the wound in Gawain's neck. But, Arthur argues, the *Gawain* poet extends the traditional concern with distinctions be-tween meaning in isolation and meaning in propositional and social context to create in Gawain a literary character who serves as a kind of sign to focus audience attention on the dangers that arise when literary interpretation is used as a mode of self-justification.

This study places an important aspect of medieval poetry in its proper historical context, and reveals the *Gawain* poet's ex-pertise in controlling ambiguity in his mate-rial in order to direct his audience towards a productive interpretative experience. It also serves to suggest a fruitful mode of analysis for other scholars working in medieval studies.

ROSS G. ARTHUR is a Canada Research Fellow in Humanities at York University.